Let There Be
Laughs

Genesis & Exodus

DARRON BAILEY JR.

WESTBOW
PRESS®
A DIVISION OF THOMAS NELSON
& ZONDERVAN

Scripture taken from the King James Version of the Bible.

WestBow Press books may be ordered through booksellers or by contacting:

WestBow Press
A Division of Thomas Nelson & Zondervan
1663 Liberty Drive
Bloomington, IN 47403
www.westbowpress.com
1 (866) 928-1240

ISBN: 978-1-5127-7416-0 (sc)
ISBN: 978-1-5127-7418-4 (hc)
ISBN: 978-1-5127-7417-7 (e)

Library of Congress Control Number: 2017901508

Print information available on the last page.

WestBow Press rev. date: 02/20/2017

I dedicate this, my first book ever to be published, to my dad, Reverend Darron Bailey Sr. You are the best father I could ever have asked for. There is no substitution. You encouraged me to pursue my dreams and helped me realize exactly what they were. Your attention to detail helped me understand how to better myself in school, in music, in writing, and even in preaching. The prayers and guidance you gave to me growing up have been engraved in my mind and my heart. You certainly bring new meaning to Proverbs 22:6: "Train up a child in the way he should go: and when he is old, he will not depart from it." I could never mention any of my talents without first mentioning how you helped me develop them.

When I'd be up late hours of the night writing this book, you'd always check up on me to see if everything was going well. You're never afraid to give me your honest opinion on my work, and that goes a long way, especially from parent to child. You are not the type of person who'd lie to me about my work, and that is why I feel such a great level of achievement when I hear you say you enjoy the ones you do. You are, and always have been, a fair father and a best friend to me. When I had no one to talk to, I had you. When I had no one to play with, I had you. When I had no one to defend me, I had you. My prayer to God is that you will have a long life and that you might have it more abundantly. I pray that you will live long on this earth and be happy with all the decisions you make. I have no regrets about any decision you have ever made for me; all your decisions shaped me into who I am today. I love you, Dad.

I also dedicate this book to my mother, Reverend Doctor Sanneth Brown. You are the greatest mother I could have ever asked for.

You are one in a million, and that is not an exaggeration. When I think of someone with the purist of hearts, you are the first person I think of. You'd read me bedtime stories when I was a toddler, and as I grew older, these stories became Bible stories. Truly you have trained me in the ways of the gospel, and I can't thank you enough. You are always lending your ear to hear my stories, you are always lending advice to make my showmanship better, and you are always lending your wisdom to keep me out of harm's way. Your love for me is beyond description. You have always discerned, decreed, and declared over all my life's endeavours. You not only demonstrated true agape parental love to me, but you also believed that all my dreams, visions, and revelations would be accomplished. Your daily prayer of authority and Holy Spirit–filled decrees over my life will always be remembered. The publishing of this book is also one of your prophetic prophesies coming to pass. The Holy Spirit prophetic anointed ministry within you is great and mighty because of the purpose God has given you. I am a million times thankful for being blessed as your son.

I will never forget your recital of Matthew 10:16: "Behold, I send you forth as sheep in the midst of wolves: be ye therefore wise as serpents, and harmless as doves." Not a day goes by that I don't remember this. I thank you for all the prayers and fasting that you've done for this book's success. I will never forget all the prayers and fasting that you did for my life—and even the ones we've done together. I am truly blessed by God to be able to say that you are my mother. My prayer for you is that you shall not die but live and declare the works of the Lord. You are a mighty force to be reckoned with, and I love you, Mom.

Finally, I'd like to dedicate this book to my grandmother, Beryl Abdulie-Gibson, or, as I like to call her, "Mommies." I love you so much and will never forget all that you have done in my life. You always ask me how I am doing whenever we meet. You are never afraid to say you love me, and you are always so generous to me. For as long as I can remember, you've always encouraged me to be happy with the love that the Lord shows me every day I wake up. You always said that that was enough reason to praise Jehovah. Nothing you've ever said to me lacked meaning, and every moment I share with you fills my heart with love, laughter, and life. I love you, Mommies.

Acknowledgments

Valarie Bryan: My protective and precious cousin, your fasting and prayers are always well received for this play. I know because everything that comes out of your mouth is sincere and from your heart. I am blessed to have you in my life and will never forget your gifts, generosity, and cooked meals. Never forget that I love you and will always remember everything you've ever done for me.

Kathleen Elliott: My always loving senior, thank you for every single word you've ever spoken into my life. You treat me as if I were your own son. I thank you so much for never leaving me out of anything you're doing, and I thank you for believing in anything I put my hands to. It is such an honor to have you so close to me. Thank you for everything. I love you very much and consider you family.

Pastor Jacqueline Stubbs: My faithful praying pastor, I will never forget all the times you watched me growing up. You have always been an adult that never speaks down to children. You treated us all like equals, and I love that about you. Thank you for always making sure that I put God first in all that I do; thank you also for your constant prayers and support.

Reverend Dorothy Richards: My always smiling godmother, your smile could light up the world. Your encouragements never fail to be right and on time. You bring such a great happiness to my life. Every time I see you, you greet me with such love and peace. You never bring bad news, and you always hold me close to your heart. Thank you for never losing faith in me and always encouraging me to be the best that I can ever be.

Reverend Paula Roach: My overflowing woman of God, you truly are a Deborah. You lead by example, you never let your adversaries bring you down, and you encourage me to do the same. You always watch my back when I need it most, and you could never be forgotten or left out. You've shown such great kindness to me. Thank you.

Ines Johnson: My prayer victor, thank you for your legitimate prayers and fasting over my life. Thank you for decreeing and declaring victory and life over me. Thank you for always showing me love and peace whenever we meet. I appreciate every moment we spend together. God bless.

Pastor Alma Aiken: My ultimate helper, where do I begin? You've constantly been praying for me and never let a day go without it. You are directly in tune with your prayer and fasting, and none of it has ever gone in vain. Thank you for helping both my mother and me in all our endeavors. Your help is never in vain.

Adia Douglas: My exciting singer, I remember the day you prophesied over my life. You said that I shall be the head and not the tail. You truly are an amazing woman. Never stop singing, because the songs and energy inside of you are radiant. Thank you for all of your prayer, fasting, and encouragements.

Late Evangelist Agnes Bodnar: My inspirational writer, though you may not be with me physically, you have never left me spiritually. I'll never forget every time you told me I was destined for greatness—not just because of my heritage but also because of who God made me specifically. Your writing was always special to me because the words and phrases you used could only have been applied to me in those situations. I love you and will never forget you.

Barbara Bodnar: My gift-giving family friend, you have such a peaceful heart and joyous smile. Thank you for all of your support, fasting, praying, and scriptures. Your generosity never goes unappreciated. Your mother would be proud.

Minister Roy Dart: My friendly and happy-hearted helper, you truly are a great person. Thank you for embracing me with open arms when we first met. Your support and constant encouragements are always in my heart as a reminder of who I am. Thank you.

Carla Wallen: My all-loving cousin, your heart is so pure and your soul so kind. You encourage me so many times when I see you. By that, I literally mean you encourage me more than once. You are great, and I appreciate all that you've done for me. I remember when you babysat me, and I'm happy to see that you're still here for me. I love you very much.

Leopold Livingston: My trustworthy worshipper, you are a great person, and your loving and positive vibe never stops uplifting my spirits. You're always encouraging me to pursue God first and trust in the Lord with all my heart. You are always positive and help in every way you can. Thank you very much. I love and appreciate you.

Marcus Miller: My best friend in the entire world, you are such a precious jewel in my life. You are the only person who can make me laugh, no matter how I feel. Whenever I am with you, it is a huge bundle of joy. Thank you for always encouraging me to pursue my dream of becoming a writer. Thank you for always fasting with me whenever I ask and without question. Thank you for always giving me your unbiased opinion of my previous work. Thank you for always being my best friend. I look forward to our many adventures and ideas in the future. I love you, Marcus.

McLaren Alphonso: My dependable teacher, words cannot describe how much of a positive influence you are to me. You taught me how to play instruments better than I ever knew how to; you always look out for me in case I'm hungry; you try your hardest to support my father, my mother, and me whenever you can. I sincerely thank you from the bottom of my heart. You've helped act in church plays and have helped me overcome difficulty playing my instruments. You are very talented and gifted by God. Please never forget that you are loved by my family and me; we thank you for everything you have done to help us.

Lyndon Charlse: My number one barber, you are more than just a barber to me. You are someone I can hold a deep conversation with about anything: faith, psychology, technology, physics, politics, film, and so on. You never turn down the opportunity to discuss something in depth, and your insight on said topics is always a breath of fresh air. Thank you for being someone who has supported many of my performances and now, I can finally say, my writing.

Ezekiel Wallen: My helpful cousin, thank you for always jumping at the opportunity to be a part of any church-related work I am doing. It always makes things easier for me, especially when I'd like to devote time to focusing on other tasks. You never let me down and always set the standard for what is expected of a youth pretty high. Even when times are stressful during productions, you keep a positive attitude and a positive outlook on what is to come. Thank you for always encouraging me to do the same. I love you and look forward to the plays you have in store in the future.

Leslie Clarke: My creative cousin, thank you for encouraging me to be a writer and thank you for always asking me how I am doing. A few words go a long way for me. You are an excellent actress, and I hope to have you in many of my plays.

Tavaughan Baisden-Smith: My virtuous soldier, you've been such a great confidant in my life. Thank you for always praying and fasting for my family and me. Never forget that you are incredibly unique and that you were made to stand out. Let your memories and kindness never fade.

Trevaughan Baisden-Smith: My fervent warrior, you're never afraid to tell the truth for what it is, and you're never afraid to read the Word. Never forget that you are not a mistake. Thank you for always being a strong and supportive person in my life, especially when it comes to God's word.

Tamiarea Mitchell-Baisden: My enthusiastic friend, thank you for believing in my writing skills and encouraging me to pursue writing in my life. It means a lot to me, and I honestly and truthfully appreciate everything you said to me.

Thea Baisden: My fellow Christ group member, you are such a genuine person. You are always positive when you speak to me and have said some of the most encouraging things to me. I couldn't possibly forget you. Thank you for your trust, thank you for your prayers, and thank you for your encouragements.

Kyle Thompson: My humble overcomer, you never cease to amaze me. Your scriptures are always perfectly timed; your words are always carefully constructed by God. Never forget that God's plan is the divine plan. Thank you for always encouraging us, the men, to fast for the Lord.

Ina Hechavarria: My generous companion, you are always happy to see me and always have something to give me. Your generosity knows no bounds. Thank you for always telling me when I am doing a great job as a leader and letting me know who I am and who I represent. Thank you so much.

Special thanks to the following:

Carrie Anthony, Marcus Baskie, Christian Buraga, Andrew Dawson, Amanda Lin, Michael Parisi, and **Tiyana Scott,** all of whom were willing to act in this play years before it was published. Thank you all for encouraging me to continue writing plays based on the Bible, and thank you for believing I could do it justice. I will never forget the first time we got together and read aloud. It was then that I knew what I wanted to do with my writing.

Todd Dickinson: My greatest drama teacher ever, you were the one who inspired the playwright in me. I've had other teachers who helped me develop my own style, but it was you who spoke one to one with me about everything involving my writing. I really looked up to you in high school, and whenever I direct plays at my church, I always ask myself, "What would Mr. Dickinson do in this situation?" That is no joke. Truly you are an inspiration in my life, and I couldn't forget everything you've done to help me become better at it. When people ask who taught me how to write and direct, I always acknowledge you first. Thank you so very much—and may God bless you with a long life and happiness.

Krista Parker: My greatest music teacher ever, you always made me laugh when I felt down. You have such a bubbly personality that always gave students a reason to come to class. You encouraged us all to embrace our dreams instead of just following what was expected of us by the school system. It's hard to find teachers who love their jobs and their students as much as you did. Not a day went by without your first asking how everyone was. I remember telling you I was writing something. Your first words were, "I'm so proud of you." I couldn't forget you here. You never stopped smiling at me and encouraging me to keep on believing in what I stand for. Thanks a million.

Cast

Characters:

(Act 1)

Thundering Voice (Sc. 4)/Gimel	Front man
Cain/Lot/Jacob	Crewman #1
The Serpent/Shin/Esau	Crewman #2
Thundering Voice (Sc. 2, 3, 5, 6, and 7)/Noah/Pharaoh	Crewman #3
Abel/Hei/Terah/Isaac	Crewman #4
Sarai/Sarah/Guardsman	Crewman #5
Adam/Nun/Abram/Abraham	Crewman #6
Eve/Angel	Crewman #7
Rebekah/Joseph	Crewman #8

(Act 2)

Bush/Thundering Voice	Front man
Moses	Crewman #1
Prisoner 2/Serpent/Israelite 1/Joshua	Crewman #2
Guard/Maid/Reuel/Jethro	Crewman #3
Prisoner 1/Aaron	Crewman #4
Puah/Miriam/Zipporah/Magician/Hur	Crewman #5
Pharoah/Amalekite 1	Crewman #6
Shiphrah/Jochebed/Sorcerer/Amalekite 2	Crewman #7
Pharaoh's daughter/Enchanter/Israelite 2	Crewman #8

Props and Costumes:

(Act 1)

Scene 1

Table
Flashlight
2 bottles of water
Mini desk
Clear sphere with an opening to pour water in—something like a fishbowl
Green stickers shaped like land with fruit on them
A model of the sun
A model of the moon and stars
Paper fish and a rubber chicken

Scene 2

2 Plants (any size)
Fake fruit (place it in one of the plants)
Blue bedsheets (at least 3)
Caveman costume (if possible)
Cave girl costume (if possible)
Serpent brown wraps (serpent brown clothing underneath)

Scene 3

1 of the water bottles used in scene 1, offstage
2 caveman costumes (if possible)
Fake fruit
Sheep wool
Stone
Washable black marker (for Cain's mark)
Cajón

Scene 4

Beard and toga (For Noah)
Ark (big enough to hold a person, lightweight, rolling mechanism for easy movement, cut out a serpent shape on one side of the ark)
Small raven
Small dove on a string or stick
Rainbow flag

Scene 5

4 different-colored togas
Tower of Babel (K'NEX if possible; have a separate top piece that needs to be constructed)

Scene 6

Water offstage
Beard and toga (for Abraham)
3 togas (for Sarah, Lot, and Terah)
Pharaoh crown
Guardsman staff
Washable black marker (for Pharaoh's plague)
Toga (for Isaac)
Table (for Isaac's sacrifice)
Fake knife (for Abraham's sacrifice)
White gown, wings, and halo (for angel)

Scene 7

4 togas (for Isaac, Rebekah, Esau, and Jacob)
Beard (for older Isaac)
Bowl (for pottage soup)
Sheep wool
Stone

White gown, wings, and halo (for angel)
Small ladder
2 pairs of boxing gloves
2 chairs
3 round # signs

Scene 8

Colorful coat (for Joseph)
Duct tape
Rope
Big well

(Act 2)

Scene 1

Nothing

Scene 2

Pharaoh costume
Handcuffs
2 blank robes (for Shiphrah and Puah)
Leather jacket and sunglasses for the guard/maid
Green baby-sized basket with blue water-looking decorations at the
bottom
2 togas for Jochebed and Miriam
Lots of jewelry (for Pharaoh's daughter)
Whip
Priest costume for Reuel
Special jewelry for Zipporah

Scene 3

Rod and toga for Moses
Toga for Aaron
Burning bush made of wrapping paper
Serpent costume from act 1, scene 2

Scene 4

3 white wizard beards
Toy snakes
Toy frogs
Toy gnats
Black and red nontoxic washable markers
Ping-Pong balls
Toy locusts
Big black blanket
Red sea made out of paper
Cloud of light
Cloud of darkness

Scene 5

3 different-colored togas for the Israelites and Hur
2 swords for Joshua to carry
Small tree for Moses to fit in pocket
Flakes of manna
Rock to put on the ground

Scene 6

Lightning bolts on a stick
Breakable tablets
Gold for Hur, Joshua, and Israelite 2
Small golden cow

Scene 7

Regular tablets
Face light (for Moses)
Veil (for Moses)

Script Legend:
() = actions
... = pauses
* = queues
- = stutters or cutoffs
{} = unsaid translation
"" = Air quotes

Important notes

Organized scripts should be offstage at all times just to be on the safe side. There must be a stand with a big printed script and a working microphone in the center far back of the stage. This is where each person will read at the designated "reads script" and "continues reading" actions.

ACT 1, SCENE 1

All of Re-creation

FRONT MAN

Hello, ladies and gentlemen. I greet you all in the name of the Father, the Son, and the blessed Holy Ghost. Now, before we start, I'd like to acknowledge the fact that though this is a comedy, a lot of the content is true and can be used as an easier way to memorize the stories of the Bible; in this case, Genesis and Exodus. When we are in church, we shouldn't have frowns on our faces. So please remember that we want you all to have a good time here and hope you have as much fun watching it as we did making it. Now, let me start by asking what's the first thing you all think about when you hear the word *Genesis*?

(*Listens and responds accordingly.*)

As we all know, Genesis was the beginning of all beginnings. In order to replicate such an outstanding introduction, I'm going to need help from the greatest Bible expert there is. So please give a warm welcome to our one and only Savior, Jesus Christ!

CREWMAN #3

(*jumping out onto stage.*)

Thank you, thank you! You're far too kind.

FRONT MAN

(*surprised.*)

Wow, umm, Jesus? I pictured you to be a little … taller.

CREWMAN #3
Huh? Oh, I'm not Jesus.

FRONT MAN
Well, where is he?
  (*He frantically looks around.*)
The show's about to start!

CREWMAN #3
Well, he told me he couldn't make it in the flesh but that he'd be with us in spirit.

FRONT MAN
B-but he has all our props! Without those, how are we going to make a good introduction?

CREWMAN #3
  (*patting shoulder and shaking head.*)
Oh, ye of little faith. If he said, "Fear not, for I am with thee," then surely he'll make a way. After all, there's a bit of him in all of us.

FRONT MAN
Wow, that's deep. Where'd you get that from?

CREWMAN #3
A little segment from Genesis 26:24. Speaking of which, we should really get started!
  (*He begins to exit the stage.*)

FRONT MAN
You're right. Wait! How are we going to do the all of re-creation scene?

CREWMAN #3

Don't worry, we'll think of something. Just do it the way you'd usually do it.

FRONT MAN

But what about the pr—

CREWMAN #3

(interrupting.)

Have faith!

(He exits the stage.)

FRONT MAN

(nervously.)

Okay, um, where do I begin? Well, as we all know, the earth took a total of six days to be created, and on the seventh day, God rested. We realized the importance of this part of the Bible, so instead of simply reading it aloud to you, we've decided to do a bit of a miniature model of what occurred during those six days. Here we go.

(He reads from the script.)

"In the beginning, God created the heaven and the earth. And the earth was without form, and void; and darkness was upon the face of the deep. And the Spirit of God moved upon the face of the waters. And God said let there be light."

(CREWMAN #3 *comes onstage and presents* FRONT MAN *with a flashlight.)*

FRONT MAN

(taking the flashlight.)

What's this?

(He sighs.)

"And there was light." (*He shines the flashlight and continues reading.*) "And God saw the light, that it was good: and God divided the light; which he called day, from the darkness; which he called night. Thus concluding the first day. And God said let there be a firmament in the midst of the waters, and divided the waters which were under the firmament from the waters above the firmament."

(CREWMAN #1 *enters stage with two bottles of water and a mini desk. He places one bottle of water on the mini desk and one underneath.*)

FRONT MAN. Really?
    (*He continues reading.*)
"And it was so. And God called the firmament heaven. Thus concluding the second day. And God said, Let the waters under the heaven be gathered together unto one place to become the sea, and let the dry land; that he soon called earth, appear. Let the earth bring forth grass, the herb yielding seed, and the fruit tree yielding fruit after his kind."

(CREWMAN #2 *enters the stage with a clear sphere and some green stickers with fruit on them. He takes the clear sphere and pours the bottom water into it and then places the stickers on the globe, disposes of the bottles, and puts the sphere under the desk.*)

FRONT MAN
Hm, not bad.
    (*He continues reading.*)
"And God saw that it was good. Thus concluding the third day. And God said, Let there be lights in the firmament of the heaven to divide the day from the night. And let them be for signs, and for seasons, and for days, and years. And God made two great lights; the greater light to rule the day, and the lesser light to rule the night: he made stars also."

CREWMAN #4

(entering the stage with a model of the sun and a model of the moon and stars; he gives a thumbs up.)

You're doing great!

(He takes the models and places them beside the sphere.)

FRONT MAN

Thanks! They totally love us!

(He continues reading.)

"Yeah. And God set them in the firmament of heaven to give light upon the earth, and God saw it was good. Thus concluding the fourth day."

Phew, we're almost done!

"And God said, Let the waters bring forth abundantly the moving creature that hath life, and fowl that may fly above the earth in the open firmament of heaven. And God created great whales, and every living creature that moveth, which the waters brought forth abundantly, after their kind, and every winged fowl after his kind."

Oh, how are we going to pull this off?

(CREWMAN #5 enters the stage with a paper fish and a rubber chicken. He places them around the sphere.)

FRONT MAN

I'm impressed!

(He continues reading.)

"And God blessed them, saying be fruitful, and multiply, and fill the waters in the seas, and let fowl multiply in the earth. Thus concluding the fifth day. And God said, Let the earth bring forth the living creature after his kind, cattle, and creeping thing, and beast of the earth after his kind: and God saw that it was good. And God said,

Let us make man (CREWMAN #6 *slowly enters the stage.*) in our image, after our likeness: and let them have …

CREWMAN #6
Pst, pst! We have a problem.

FRONT MAN
What is it?

CREWMAN #6
We're all out of props for this scene.

FRONT MAN
Out of props? Out of props! How on earth can we be out of props? (*All other* CREWMEN *enter stage and complain about different reasons all at once, creating a cluster of noise.*)

FRONT MAN
All right, all right! (*The* CREWMEN *go quiet.*) Does anyone have any other ideas for how we can do this?
    (*No one raises a hand.*)
Nobody?

CREWMAN #6
Oh, I do! Everyone huddle up.
    (*All* CREWMEN *huddle and listen to* CREWMAN #6's *idea.*)

CREWMAN #6
Break on three—one, two, three!

ALL CREWMEN
Break!
    (*They exit the stage.*)

FRONT MAN
Wait, what do I do?

CREWMAN #6
Just start that line over again.

FRONT MAN
(*continues reading.*)
Okay, then. "And God said, Let us make man in our image, after our likeness: and let them have dominion over the fish of sea, and over the fowl of the air, and over the cattle, and over all the earth, and over every creeping thing that creepeth upon the earth. So God created (*All* CREWMEN *carry* CREWMAN *#6 from offstage toward the table with the other items.*) man in his own image, in the image of God."
(CREWMAN *#6 smiles gleefully.*)

FRONT MAN
(*shaking his head.*)
You can't be serious.
(*He sighs and continues reading.*)
"He gave man all that was on the earth. Thus concluding the sixth day! And He rested on the seventh day from all his work which he had made!"
(*The* FRONT MAN *exits the stage.*)

ACT 1, SCENE 2

The Adam Family

(*All* CREWMEN *except #3 exit the stage with any props already onstage and gather props for the next scene. They return to stage with the props at each * and exit after.*)

CREWMAN #3
(*stepping downstage.*)
Yes, yes, yes.
(*He reads from the script.*)
"It was the sixth day that God created one of his greatest creations using nothing but the dust of the earth. He shaped him, and then breathed the breath of life into his nostrils, and then became he a living soul, named Adam. After God's rest, He planted a garden eastward in Eden; and there he put the man whom he had formed. * God grew every tree that is pleasant to the sight, and good for food; the tree of life also in the midst of the garden, and the tree of knowledge of good and evil. * He then made four rivers: Pison, Gihon, Hiddekel, and Euphrates." Now that our set is done.
(*Looks behind and snaps back with a smile.*)
What little we have. Let's give a round of applause to our ... Adam!

ADAM
(*from offstage.*)
I'm not ready yet!
(*He throws out his pants from offstage.*)

CREWMAN #3

(*shocked, rushes to pants and throws them back offstage.*)
Dude, put your clothes back on!

ADAM

from offstage. But I'm Adam, remember? Aren't I supposed to be naked?

CREWMAN #3

(*still shocked.*)
Well, yes, but the last thing we want is for our audience to leave! Just be Adam with your clothes on.

ADAM,

(*jumping out onto the stage in a caveman costume.*)
How do I look?

CREWMAN #3

(*smiling.*)
It's an improvement. Anyway, Adam, do you remember what God told you?

ADAM

About what?

CREWMAN #3

About those two trees over there.

ADAM

Oh, yes. God told me of every tree of the garden I may eat freely. But of the Tree of Knowledge of Good and Evil, I shalt not eat: for in the day I eatest thereof, I will surely die. And then he let me name all his beautiful animals.

CREWMAN #3
Indeed he did. Do you remember what happened afterward?

ADAM
No, not quite.

CREWMAN #3
Oh, yes, of course. You were in a deep sleep. It was then that God took one of your ribs and—

ADAM
(*shocked.*)
He did what?

CREWMAN #3
    (*knocks on Adam's head.*) *Adam falls down to sleep.*
Go to sleep. As I was saying …
    (*He continues reading.*)
It was then that God took one of Adam's ribs, and closed up the flesh instead thereof; and from the rib, which God had taken from man, made he a woman he soon called Lilith.

FRONT MAN
    (*He returns from offstage.*)
Lilith?

CREWMAN #3
Yeah, wasn't that the name of Adam's wife?

FRONT MAN
Maybe in the *Midrashic* text or in *Jewish mythology* but definitely not in the Bible!

CREWMAN #3, *shocked, turns to audience.*
Oh, I am so sorry!
    (*He exits stage.*)

FRONT MAN. Clearly someone didn't study their Bible. Anyway, using Adam's rib, God created woman And brought her unto Adam.

EVE, *jumps onstage in cave girl costume.*

ADAM, *wakes up.*
Huh, what happened?
    (*Sees Eve; gets up in awe*)
This is now bone of my bones, and flesh of my flesh: she shall be called woman, because she was taken out of man.

ADAM and EVE
    (*They exit hand in hand; Eve returns at * and sits down*)

FRONT MAN
    (*Reads script*)
And Adam called the woman to be his wife. Life was good for them in the Garden of Eden, nice cool breeze, beautiful animal life, and good health care. * But it wasn't long until something came along and ruined it. Now the serpent was more subtle than any beast of the field which God had made.

EVE
    (*Looking around gracefully*)

THE SERPENT
    (*Enters stage crawling and squirming on the ground*)

EVE and FRONT MAN
    (*Stares at the serpent and face palm*)

THE SERPENT

(*Looks up and sees them*)

Oh, like you had any better ideasssssss!

FRONT MAN

Please don't tell me that's part of the ark …

THE SERPENT

Okay I won't tell you this is part of the ark.

EVE

You do know that the serpent wasn't on the ground until *after* we were banished, right?

THE SERPENT

Oh! Now she tells me …

(*Stands up*)

All right. Do that line over.

FRONT MAN

(*He shakes head and continues reading.*)

The serpent approached Eve in the midst of the garden.

THE SERPENT

Yea, hath God said, Ye shall not eat of every tree of the garden?

EVE

We may eat of the fruit of the trees of the garden: But of the fruit of the tree which is in the midst of the garden, God hath said, Ye shall not eat of it, neither shall ye touch it, lest ye die.

THE SERPENT

Ye shall not surely die: For God doth know that in the day ye eat thereof, then your eyes shall be opened, and ye shall be as gods, knowing good and evil.

EVE

Really?

THE SERPENT

Would I lie to you?
(*Exits stage*)

EVE

Okay.
(*Picks up fake fruit from the tree, bites it, and opens her eyes wide*)

ADAM

(*Enters stage, shocked*)
Eve!

EVE

(*Rushes over to Adam*)
Adam! Adam! You have to try this fruit!

ADAM

Where'd you get it?

EVE

Oh, never mind that! Just eat some.

ADAM

(*Bites fruit and opens eyes widely*)

FRONT MAN

And the eyes of them both were opened, and they knew that they were naked.

ADAM and EVE

(*Look at each other slowly, cover their private parts, and scream at the audience*)

FRONT MAN

And they heard the voice of God walking in the garden in the cool of the day: and Adam and his wife hid themselves from the presence of God amongst the trees of the garden. And God called unto Adam.

THUNDERING VOICE

Where art thou?

ADAM

I heard thy voice in the garden, and I was afraid because I was naked; I hid myself.

THUNDERING VOICE

Who told thee that thou wast naked? Hast thou eaten of the tree whereof I commanded thee that thou shouldest not eat?

ADAM

The woman whom thou gavest to be with me gave me of the tree, and I did eat.

THUNDERING VOICE

What is this that thou hast done?

EVE

The serpent beguiled me, and I did eat.

THE SERPENT
(*Enters stage*)
Hey now! Don't go blaming me!

THUNDERING VOICE
Because thou hast done this, thou art cursed above all cattle, and above every beast of the field; upon thy belly shalt thou go, and dust shalt thou eat all the days of thy life.

THE SERPENT
Aw man ...
(*Goes to the ground and pulls itself to exit stage*)

CREWMAN #8
(*Starts clearing stage*)

FRONT MAN
And God told Eve that he would greatly multiply her sorrow, told Adam that the ground he walks on is cursed for his sake. Clearly God was angry with them. So in order to prevent Adam or Eve from taking fruit from the tree of life, which would allow them to live eternally, he banished them from their paradise, the Garden of Eden, and placed a cherub and a flaming sword that turned every way, to keep the way of the tree of life.

EVE
Wow, this really bites ...

ADAM
Yeah, but let's look on the bright side. I finally thought of a name for you.

EVE
Really? What is it?

ADAM
(*Opens mouth ready to speak; slowly looks at* FRONT MAN)

FRONT MAN
(*Whispers*)
Eve …

ADAM
(*Smiles and looks at her*)
Eve!

ADAM and EVE
(*Exit stage*)

FRONT MAN
And Adam knew Eve his wife; and she conceived, and bare two children, Cain and Abel.
(*Exits stage*)

CAIN and ABEL
(*Enter stage with fruit and sheep wool at respectful *s)

ACT 1, SCENE 3

Civilization–Cain

CREWMAN #5

(*Enters stage*)

Now.

(*Reads script*)

Cain and Abel were like any other siblings. * One was stronger, * one was smarter, and of course one was favored over the other. In this case, it was God who favored Abel, the keeper of the sheep, over Cain, the tiller of the ground. This was because the firstborn, Cain, brought forth fruit of the ground sparingly, while his younger brother, Abel, brought forth the firstlings of his flock and of the fat thereof wholeheartedly. Cain wasn't very happy …

CAIN

(*Slyly walks over to Abel*)

Hey there, little bro.

(*Places arm around Abel*)

What do you say you and I go out into the field?

ABEL

(*Thinks*)

I don't know …

CAIN

Oh, come on. I have something special there for you.

ABEL
Okay!

CAIN and ABEL
(*Walk in a circle*)

CAIN
(*Releases Abel and reaches for stone from back pocket*)
Wow, we're finally here in the field.

ABEL
Yup. What was it you wanted to show me?

CAIN
(*Holds stone up high*)
Your grave!
(*Hits Abel in the head and makes him fall*)
Strike!

THUNDERING VOICE
Where is Abel?

CAIN
(*Looks towards the sky*)
I know not; am I my brother's keeper?

THUNDERING VOICE
(*Angrily*)
What hast thou done? The voice of thy brother's blood crieth unto me from the ground. And now art thou cursed from the earth, which hath opened her mouth to receive thy brother's blood from thy hand; When thou tillest the ground, it shall not henceforth yield unto thee her strength; a fugitive and a vagabond shalt thou be in the earth.

CAIN

My punishment is greater than I can bear.
   (*Marks forehead with marker at **)

CREWMAN #5

   (*Continues reading*)
Because of Cain's fear of being slain by the first person that found him, * God set a mark upon Cain and said unto him: whosoever slayeth Cain, vengeance shall be taken on him sevenfold. Then Cain left the presence of God, dwelt in the land of Nod, on east of Eden, met his wife and had many, many, many children. Thus concluding the story of Cain and—

CAIN

Wait, what? That's it?

CREWMAN #5

Well, yeah. There's a lot of genealogy and a big family tree that we don't have time for.

CAIN

   (*Walks towards* CREWMAN #5)
But what about the civilization rap?

CREWMAN #5

We had to cut that out 'cause we figured everyone in the audience probably already knows that.

CAIN

Psh! Yeah, right!
   (*Walks towards audience*)
Does anyone in here know the name of Cain's wife? Go ahead and shout it out if you do! Come on, someone shout it out!

(*If audience cooperates, great. If not then move on.*)
See, no one in here knows. So I guess you know what that means.
Give me a beat, Adam.

(*Takes microphone from script reading area*)

ADAM
(Plays cajón)
Civilization—Cain rap

Cain: Was it Awan? Aklia? Why worry, fret, or strife?
'Cause all that really matters is I found myself a wife!
The land of Nod was tiny, and society was shrinking;
We got busy and had Enoch, but it's not the one you're thinking.
Enoch had Irad, and Irad had Mahujael.
Not much is known about him, but we know he had Methuselah.

Frnt: What did I say about doing the rap?
You guys keep this up, I'm gonna give you a slap.

Cain: Don't worry, man, they'll love it. It'll just take a sec!
I was just about to say Methuselah had Lamech.
Now, Lamech had two wives named Adah and Zillah
He couldn't choose between 'em. Whoda thought he was a dealah?

Cre5: Jabal and Jubal were the two sons of Adah.

Frnt: No, not you too!

Cain: C'mon, what's the mattah?

Cre5: Zillah had Naamah and Tubal-cain.

Frnt: With a name like, that I'm sure he was a pain!

Cain: Ha-ha, very funny. Let's not argue with each other.
Instead let's talk about how my folks gave me a brother.
Not Abel, of course. God gave my folks a third.
Seth was his name, at least that's what I've heard.

Cre5: Seth married Azura, and they had a son named Enos.
Uh … um … my favorite planet's Venus?

Cain: I'll take it from here. Enos begot Cainan.
I bet you didn't know he lived to be nine hundred and ten.
Cain: Mahalaleel, then Jared, and then the special Enoch.
See, I've saved you some time, man. Chill.

Frnt: Well, don't you rock.

Cain: Methuselah the oldest man, Lamech the other one.
And finally there's Noah.

Frnt: And now the rap is done?

Cain: We hope you all enjoyed it, 'cause writing it was a pain.
We hope you all remember the Civilization-Cain rap!

ALL EXCEPT CREWMAN #8

(*Exit stage making sure the microphone is put back by the script reading area*)

ACT 1, SCENE 4

Floody Massacre

CREWMAN #8
(Enters stage. If audience is clapping, do a dramatic conductor stop. If not, then disregard this. Reads script.)
And God saw that the wickedness of man was great in the earth, and that every imagination of the thoughts of his heart was only evil continually. And it grieved him at his heart. And God said, I will destroy man whom I have created from the face of the earth; both man, and beast, and the creeping thing, and the fowls of the air; for it repenteth me that I have made them. But Noah found grace in the eyes of God. These are the generations of Noah.

NOAH
(Enters stage. Walks around aimlessly.)

THUNDERING VOICE
Noah!

NOAH
(Startled)
Ah.

THUNDERING VOICE
Awe, indeed.

NOAH
You sound different …

THUNDERING VOICE
Never mind that. The end of all fresh is come before me; for the earth is filled with violence through them; and, behold I will destroy them with the earth. Make thee an ark of gopher wood; rooms shalt thou make in the ark, and shalt pitch it within and without with pitch.

NOAH
(Reaches offstage)
You mean like this?
(Pulls ark from offstage)

THUNDERING VOICE
That depends. Is it three hundred by thirty cubits, with a window, a door at the side, and three different stories?

NOAH
Uh …
(Checks the ark)
Yeah.

THUNDERING VOICE
(Laughs)
Oh, Noah. So prepared. Surely there will be a special place for you in heaven. Now, about that ark …

NOAH
What did you have in mind for it?

THUNDERING VOICE
I do bring a flood of waters upon the earth, to destroy all flesh, wherein is the breath of life, from under heaven.

NOAH
(*Places hand by mouth as though he were whispering*)
It's Cain's children, isn't it?

THUNDERING VOICE
Goodness gracious me. Yes! How did you know?

NOAH
Anyone could tell just by looking. The way they fight each other. The way they lie about everything. How they eat with their mouths open!

THUNDERING VOICE
How they tried to build a tower to see heaven. Ugh. It's unbearable.

NOAH
I don't remember anything about a tower.

THUNDERING VOICE
Oh, yes, that's right. That hasn't happened yet. You'll know it when you see it, though. Oh, wait—no, you won't. Anyway, what was I saying?

NOAH
Something about a flood.

THUNDERING VOICE
Oh, yes. Thou shalt come into the ark, thou and thy sons, and thy wife, and thy sons' wives with thee. And of every living thing of all flesh, two of every sort shalt thou bring into the ark, to keep them alive with thee; they shall be male and female.

NOAH

I shall.

(*Exits stage with ark. Crewmen #4 and #7 return to stage, pushing Noah in the ark at* *)

CREWMAN #8

(*Continues reading*)

Thus did Noah; according to all that God commanded him, so did he. And it came to pass after seven days, * that the waters of the flood were upon the earth. And every living substance was destroyed which was upon the face of the ground.

(*Gestures to crewmen to turn the ark around* [the ark has a big serpent shape cut out of it])

And he sent forth a raven, which went forth to and fro, until the waters were dried up from off the earth.

NOAH

(*Releases raven by throwing it offstage*)

CREWMAN #8

(*Continues reading*)

Also he sent forth a dove from him, to see if the waters were abated from off the face of the ground.

NOAH

(*Releases dove*)

CREWMAN #7

(*Carries dove away from ark gracefully*)

CREWMAN #8

(*Continues reading*)

But the dove found no rest for the sole of her foot, and she returned unto him into the ark.

CREWMAN #7

(*Returns dove to ark gracefully*)

CREWMAN #8

(*Continues reading*)
In forty days, it stopped raining. After one hundred and fifty days, the ground finally dried and Noah's ark came to rest on Mount Ararat.

NOAH

(*Exits ark*)
Phew. Now that's what I call a road trip.
(*Looks up to the sky*)
I will show you my thanks by making a sacrifice.

THUNDERING VOICE

I will not again curse the ground any more for man's sake; for the imagination of man's heart is evil from his youth; neither will I again smite any more everything living, as I have done.

CREWMAN #4

(*Waves rainbow flag*)

NOAH

(*Sees rainbow*)
Um. What is that?

THUNDERING VOICE

I do set my bow in the cloud, and it shall be for a token of a covenant between me and the earth.

(*Sarcastically*)
But it won't be long before that changes completely.

NOAH and CREWMEN #4 and #8
(*Exit stage with ark*)

ACT 1, SCENE 5

Bablio Brothers

CREWMAN #7

(*Reads script*)

Noah lived for 950 years before he died. His family multiplied and it didn't take long for people to start doing unholy things. I can't be the only one seeing a pattern here. You see as people journeyed from the east and dwelt in the land of Shinar, they hatched a devious plan.

(*Exits stage*)

GIMEL

(*Enters stage melodramatically*)

Brother Shin!

SHIN

(*Enters stage melodramatically*)

Yes, brother?

GIMEL

How art thou?

SHIN

Fine, thank you. Brother Nun!

NUN

(*Enters stage melodramatically*)

Yes, brother?

SHIN
How art thou?

NUN
Fine, thank you. Brother Hei!

HEI
(*Enters stage melodramatically*)
Yes, brother?

NUN
How art thou?

HEI
Fine, thank you. Brother Gimel, how art thou?

GIMEL
Just peachy. Now, brothers, gather your ears.

ALL
(*Huddle in*)

GIMEL
Let us build us a city and a tower, whose top may reach unto heaven; and let us make us a name, lest we be scattered abroad upon the face of the whole Earth!

SHIN
What an excellent idea, brother!

NUN
Surely one of your greatest!

HEI
(Stops huddling)
I disagree ... I doubt God would be happy about that.

GIMEL, SHIN, and NUN
(Stop huddling)
Hei!

GIMEL
Hey, hey, Hei. What troubles you so?

HEI
Have you not heard of the God that dwells in heaven?

SHIN
Everyone has heard of that God.

HEI
Dost thou truly believe that He would be satisfied with us?

NUN
What makest thou think otherwise?

GIMEL
(Slyly puts arm around)
Hei, look at it this way. The whole world will soon look up to you, and at you, sitting on your own personal throne in heaven.

HEI
I ... am uncertain. I mean, I don't think anyone will ever remember our names.

GIMEL
(Walks away slowly)

All right, then.
(*Turns around aggressively*)
Off with his head!

SHIN and NUN
(*Grab Hei and begin to drag him offstage*)

HEI
(*Upset*)
Oh, not again!
(*They both exit stage.*)
Ah!
(*Dies*)

SHIN and NUN
(*Enter stage*)
It's done, brother.

GIMEL
(*Mockingly*)
Don't worry, Hei. We'll be up there soon.

SHIN
How do you suppose we build this tower?

NUN
Indeed. It would take us a year to gather the materials alone.

GIMEL
Worry not, brothers.
(*Takes out Tower of Babel from offstage*)

Fortunately, I have already constructed most of it. But due to our poor brother's … accident, we are forced to recruit a member of the audience.

ALL
(*Slowly look towards audience*)

GIMEL
(*Steps downstage*)
We require assistance from one very able person, someone who is capable of assembling a nice top piece for our tower.
(*Do a show of hands*)
Thank you, thank you. Now, may I ask your name?
(*Listens to name*)
All right [insert name here], you must assemble the top of our tower using only these pieces.
(*Directs attention to Shin and Nun*)

SHIN and NUN
(*Exit stage and return with K'NEX*)

GIMEL
(*To audience*)
The rest of you may cheer them on.
(*To person*)
You may begin when ready.

GIMEL, SHIN, and NUN
(*Cheer person on very dramatically*)
(*Discuss amongst each other how well they're doing*)

SHIN
(*After person is complete, grabs the tower piece and holds it up*)

Truly this is magnificent!

NUN

(*Grabs tower piece from Shin*)
Yes, of course! There is none like it.

GIMEL

(*Grabs tower piece from Nun*)
'Tis true, which is why I've decided to place it on top.
(*To person*)
You may leave now.
(*Walks towards Tower in slow motion*)

SHIN

(Stands at soldier-esque attention position)

NUN

(*Hums a nice tune*)

THUNDERING VOICE

(*While the above is happening*)
Behold, the people is one, and this they begin to do: and now nothing will be restrained from them, which they have imagined to do. Go to, let us go down, and there confound their language, that they may not understand one another's speech. Shazaam!

GIMEL

(*Realizes the tower is too high; turns around to ask brother for help*)
It seems as though the tower is too high. I am in need of assistance, brothers.

SHIN

Qu'est-ce que tu dit?   {What did you say?}

GIMEL
What was that?

NUN
(*Counting parts of the tower*)
Ūnus.   {One}
(*Confused, slowly*)
Duo, Trēs.   {Two, Three}
(*Shocked*)
Quattuor, Quīnque. Ah!   {Four, Five.}

GIMEL
(*To brothers*)
What on earth are you …
(*To audience*)
"Babel-ing" on about?

SHIN
Que se passe-t-il?   {What is going on?}

NUN
(*In desperation*)
Sex, septem, octō, novem!   {Six, Seven, Eight, Nine!}

GIMEL
Oh, forget it!
(*Exits stage*)

NUN
(*Sadly*)
Decem!   {Ten!}
(*Exits stage running*)

SHIN

(*Grabs Tower of Babel*)

Regardez comme je suis fort.   {Look how strong I am.}

(*Exits stage with Tower of Babel*)

CREWMAN #7

(*Enters stage and reads script*)

Therefore is the name of the tower called Babel; because God did there confound the language of all the earth: and from thence did He scatter them abroad upon the face of all the earth.

ACT 1, SCENE 6

Father Abram

CREWMAN #7

(*Continues reading*)

Four thousand nine hundred and sixty-five years later, Abram was born. And Abram's wife was named Sarai. Under the guidance of his father, Terah; Abram; his nephew, Lot; his wife, Sarai; and his brothers, Nahor and Haran, travelled to the land of Canaan.

TERAH

(*Enters stage galloping as if he were on a horse*)

This way, son.

ABRAM

(*Enters stage galloping as if he were on a horse*)

Right behind you, Father! The rest of the family is following our trail.

LOT

(*Enters stage sprinting behind Terah and Abram*)

Could I not have gotten a horse as well?

TERAH

Preposterous. You are young, Lot. The running is good for your bones. It'll keep you pure, just, holy, and—

LOT

(*Fake muffles*)

Idol worshipper.

TERAH
   (*Stops horse*)
Whoa, I'm sorry. What was that?

ABRAM
   (*Stops horse, gets off horse, and rushes to Lot*)
Whoa, Father, I assure you my nephew's simply thinking out loud.
The heat must be getting to him.
   (*Looks at Lot*)
Right, Lot?

LOT
   (*Sighs*)
Right.

TERAH
Very well, then.
   (*Gets off horse*)
Since you are clearly tired, you may take my horse.

ABRAM
   (*Looks at Lot*)
What do you say?

LOT
Thank you, Grandpa Terah.
   (*Jumps on horse and gallops away*)

TERAH
   (*Watches as Lot gallops offstage*)
Aw, youthfulness. How I miss the days ...

(*Holds chest*)

Ugh.

ABRAM

(*Rushes to Terah's aid*)

Father, are you all right?

TERAH

Abram, I don't think I'm going to make it to Canaan.

(*Falls into Abram's arms*)

But before I go, I must ask if I have to die in every scene I'm in!

(*Dies*)

ABRAM

No, Father!

(*Looks at the sky*)

And we were only three seconds away!

(*Puts body down*)

Seriously, look.

(*Takes five steps stage left and looks at audience*)

Voilà! I'm in Canaan … Wait. No, this is still Haran.

THUNDERING VOICE

Abram!

ABRAM

Awe.

THUNDERING VOICE

'Tis I. Get thee out of thy country, and from thy kindred, and from thy father's house, unto a land that I will shew thee: And I will make of thee a great nation, and I will bless thee, and ma …

ABRAM
  (*Pondering*)
Wait a minute.

THUNDERING VOICE
Yes, what is it?

ABRAM
You sound different.

THUNDERING VOICE
And I will bless thee, and make thy name great; and thou shalt be
a blessing: And I will bless them that bless thee, and curse him that
curseth thee: and in thee shall all families of the earth be blessed.

ABRAM
I shall do as thy commands.
  (*Exits stage*)

CREWMAN #7
  (*Continues reading*)
So Abram departed, as God had spoken unto him; and Abram took
his wife Sarai and his brother's son Lot; and they went forth to go into
the land of Canaan; and into the land of Canaan they came. Then
Abram built an alter unto a mountain on the east of Bethel. Abram,
Sarai, and Lot continued their journey south and soon enough arrived
in Egypt.

ABRAM, SARAI, PHARAOH, and GUARDSMAN
  (*Enter stage: Abram and Sarai stage left; Pharaoh and Guardsman
stage right*)

ABRAM
Behold now, Sarai, I know that thou art a fair woman to look upon:
Therefore it shall come to pass, when the Egyptians shall see thee,
that they shall say, This is his wife: and they will kill me.

SARAI
What do you suppose we do instead?

ABRAM
Say that thou art my sister.

SARAI
    (*Flirtatiously gasps*)
You want me to lie for you?
    (*Flirtatiously*)
When did you become so daring?

ABRAM
Well, you know, sometimes a man's got to do what a man's got to do.
    (*They approach Pharaoh*)

PHARAOH
Hello there! May I ask if it hurt?

SARAI
Did what hurt?

PHARAOH
    (*Flirtatiously*)
When you fell from heaven.

GUARDSMAN
Good one, sire.
    (*Goes for a high five*)

PHARAOH
(*Glances at guardsman repulsively*)

GUARDSMAN
(*Puts hand down in shame*)

PHARAOH
Who is this fair woman?

SARAI
I am …
(*Looks at Abram quickly*)
… his sister.

PHARAOH
Excellent! Come to my house immediately.
(*Grabs Sarai and steps offstage while Sarai is still onstage*)
Ah! What's happening?
(*Returns from offstage with a visible mark*)
What is this that thou hast done to me? Why didst thou not tell me that she was thy wife? Now I am plagued! You!
(*Points to guardsman*)
Take them away.

GUARDSMAN
Yes, sire!
(*Takes Abram and Sarai offstage; returns from offstage*)
They are out of Egypt now, sire.

PHARAOH
I cannot believe those people.

GUARDSMAN

They're repulsive, sire, utterly repulsive.

PHARAOH

Quite a fair woman though wouldn't you say?

GUARDSMAN

Oh, truly, sire! Most certainly.
  (*Goes for high five again*)

PHARAOH

  (*Looks at guardsman distastefully; exits stage*)

GUARDSMAN

  (*Follows Pharaoh with hand held high; exits stage*)

CREWMAN #7

  (*Continues reading*)

Abram and Sarai went out of Egypt and into the south. And Abram said unto Lot, Let there be no strife, I pray thee, between me and thee; for we are brethren. Abram dwelled in the land of Canaan, and Lot dwelled in the cities of the plain, and pitched his tent towards a wicked place called Sodom ... then kings changed, lots of people died, Abram left Canaan, had a child named Ishmael to his wife's maid Hagar by his wife's command, had a covenant sealed by God, a name change along with his wife, and was told that the now "Sarah" would soon have a child for him. We're in Genesis eighteen now, for those of you who are wondering.

ABRAHAM

  (*Enters stage; strolls around*)

THUNDERING VOICE
Abraham.

ABRAHAM
(*Doesn't notice*)

THUNDERING VOICE
Abraham.

ABRAHAM
(*Doesn't notice*)

THUNDERING VOICE
Abraham!

ABRAHAM
(*Looks up and then points at himself*)

THUNDERING VOICE
Yes, you.

ABRAHAM
Oh yeah! I forgot. I'm still getting used to the new name.

THUNDERING VOICE
I came to tell you that I plan on destroying Sodom and Gomorrah.

ABRAHAM
Wilt thou also destroy the righteous with the wicked? Peradventure there be fifty righteous within the city: wilt thou also destroy and not spare the place for the fifty righteous that are therein?

THUNDERING VOICE
If I find in Sodom and Gomorrah fifty righteous men within the city, then I will spare all the place for their sakes.

ABRAHAM
Peradventure there shall lack five of the fifty righteous: wilt thou destroy all the city for *lack of* five?

THUNDERING VOICE
How about this? If I find forty-five righteous men, I will not destroy Sodom and Gomorrah.

ABRAHAM
Okay. Um …

THUNDERING VOICE
Yes, Abraham?

ABRAHAM
Suppose there are only thirty righteous men? Wilt thou still destroy it?

THUNDERING VOICE
    (*Sigh*)
If I find thirty righteous men, I will not destroy it.

ABRAHAM
Thank you. But, um, suppose there be only twenty righteous men.

THUNDERING VOICE
Really?

ABRAHAM
Be not angry at me, for I am but dust and ashes.

THUNDERING VOICE
Fine. If I find at least twenty righteous men, I will not destroy it.

ABRAHAM
How about ten?

THUNDERING VOICE
Abraham …

ABRAHAM
(Begs)
Ten and that's it.

THUNDERING VOICE
Ten it is. I already know the true number of righteous men anyway.

CREWMAN #7
(Continues reading)
In the end, God destroyed the lands of Sodom and Gomorrah, after sending two angels to save Lot, of course. For there were no righteous men in that land. Do you remember that thing Abraham did with the Pharaoh of Egypt? Telling Sarah to tell him that she was Abraham's sister? Well, yeah, they did that again, only this time with Abimelech the king of Gerar. God told Abimelech the truth in a dream and soon enough they were banished from Gerar. Okay, now my favorite part! Sarah gave birth to a boy named Isaac. She later forced Abraham to cast out his other son, Ishmael.
(Snickers)
Remember that guy? Yeah, well, God agreed with Sarah and soon enough Ismael and his mother, Hagar, were cast out from their sights. But don't worry, they lived happily ever elsewhere! And it came to pass after these things, that God did tempt Abraham, and said unto him:

(*Exits stage*)

THUNDERING VOICE
Abraham.

ABRAHAM
Here I am.

THUNDERING VOICE
Take now thy son, thine only son Isaac, whom thou lovest, and get thee into the land of Moriah; and offer him there for a burnt offering upon one of the mountains.

ABRAHAM
As you command. I shall awaken early, saddle my ...
      (*Looks at audience and winks*)
... donkey, and head to the mountain in Moriah. But first ...
      (*Shouting*)
... Isaac! Isaac? Isaac!

CREWMAN #4
      (*from offstage*)
I'm not coming out there!

ABRAHAM
      (*To audience*)
One moment, please.
      (*Runs offstage*)
What's the problem?

CREWMAN #4
I die in every scene I'm in! Get someone else to do it!

ABRAHAM
What are you talking about? You're about to play Isaac!

CREWMAN #4
Yes, and you're about to sacrifice him. So I don't want to do it!

ABRAHAM
(*Returns to stage*)
Finally we've arrived at Mount Moriah …

CREWMAN #4
(*From offstage*)
I'm not coming out.

ABRAHAM
Oh, Isaac! Isaac! Where art thou Isaac?

CREWMAN #4
(*Enters stage in Isaac's costume and holding a table*)
Fine, let's get this over with.
(*Lies on table*)

ABRAHAM
Aw, there you are, Isaac. Where's the rope?

ISAAC
Why bother? You're just going to kill me anyway.

ABRAHAM
(*Draws knife and slowly descends arms*)

ISAAC
(*Sarcastically*)
Oh, look, a knife. Why am I not surprised?

(*Closes eyes*)

ANGEL
(*Stops Abraham's arms*)

ABRAHAM and ISAAC
(*Look at angel*)
Huh?

ANGEL
Lay not thine hand upon the lad, neither do thou anything unto him: for now I know that thou fearest God.

ISAAC
(*Gets on knees and holds angel*)
Oh, thank you, thank you, thank you!

FRONT MAN
(*Enters stage*)
So God gave Abraham a lamb and blessed Abraham for remaining faithful to Him and never questioning his order. Thus concludes the story of Abraham.

ABRAHAM and ISAAC
Amen!
(*Exit stage*)

ACT 1, SCENE 7

Twinception

FRONT MAN

(*Reads script*)

After his mother died at the youthful age of 127, Isaac's father Abraham was stricken in age. But before he died Abraham made sure his son married a non-Canaanite woman.

(*Shakes head*)

Parents, am I right? So he sent forth his servant to look for a woman chosen by God's angel and made his servant swear under oath that he would do so. Abraham's Servant went into the land of Mesopotamia, unto the city of Nahor, and chose a woman named Rebekah.

REBEKAH

(*Enters stage. Poses at first *, prayer hands at second *, snaps fingers with attitude at third **)

FRONT MAN

(*Continues reading*)

After she let the servant drink from her water pitcher he knew she was the one for Isaac. Could you imagine that? But don't worry. * She was very fair to look upon, * a virgin, neither had any man known her * . The servant told Rebekah his reason for coming and voila she married Isaac!

ISAAC

(*Enters the stage*)

Who's this lovely lady?

ISAAC and REBEKAH
(*Hold each other's hands and exit stage*)

FRONT MAN
(*Continues reading*)
After Abraham got remarried to a woman named Keturah, he had six other sons and died soon after. Everyone attended the funeral ... even Ishmael! Remember that guy? Anyway, back to Isaac and Rebekah. At the age of forty, Isaac and Rebekah married and Rebekah was pregnant with two children. After wrestling in the womb, the strongest of the two was born first. Let's give it up for Esau!

ESAU
(*Enters stage flexing*)

FRONT MAN
And the "muscularly challenged" one was born after. Give it up for Jacob!

JACOB
(*Enters stage and speaks to* FRONT MAN)
"Muscularly challenged"? Puh!
(*To audience with hand around mouth as though he's whispering*)
Tell that to the angel I fight later on.

FRONT MAN
But not only were these two brothers—they were also ... twin brothers!

ESAU AND JACOB

(*Look at each other surprised and mime each other movements; address audience*)

This isn't going to end well.

FRONT MAN

(*Continues reading*)

Esau grew to become a cunning hunter, while his brother Jacob was a plain man dwelling in tents. Isaac favored Esau, and Rebekah favored Jacob. One day when Jacob was making soup, Esau returned home exhausted.

ESAU

(*Yawns and stretches*)

Oh, what a day! All that hunting has tuckered me out. Not that you'd know anything about that brother ... I am starving!

JACOB

Oh, I prepared something special for you. Wait right here.

(*Grabs bowl from offstage*)

How about some soup?

ESAU

Don't mind if I do.

(*Reaches for bowl*)

JACOB

(*Snatches it away*)

You can have it ... but you have to give me something first.

ESAU

Ugh ... What do you want?

JACOB
(*Ponders*)
Hm … How about … your birthright?

ESAU
Absolutely not!

JACOB
Okay, fine … I guess I'll just have to eat this soup all by myself.
(*Tilts bowl towards mouth*)

ESAU
No, wait! Surely there must be something else you'd be willing to trade!

JACOB
I'm sorry, but I can't hear you over the smell of this delicious soup! I added some dumplings to the usual mix. Some olives …
(*Walks around Esau*)
… roasted chicken, soft beans, herbs …

ESAU
(*Licks lips and frowns*)
Um … Hm.

JACOB
And oh! What's that?
(*Sniffs*)
Is that … cow foot?

ESAU
Okay, okay. I am at the point to die: and what profit shall this birthright do to me?

(*Begs Jacob*)

I swear to you this day and I sell you my birthright!
(*Grabs bowl and begins to eat while exiting stage*)

FRONT MAN

(*Continues reading*)

When the family moved away to the land of Gerar, Isaac told King Abimelech that his wife Rebekah was his sister … Sound familiar? The only difference this time is that they were not banished for it. Years passed and Isaac was on the brink of death, but he had one more thing to do before he died. Bless his favorite son, Esau … but not all goes according to plan.

REBEKAH

(*Enters stage with sheep wool; rushes to Jacob*)

Jacob! Jacob! Your father's planning on blessing Esau before he dies. He just sent Esau out to make fresh soup for him. Here, put this hair on your arms.
(*Gives Jacob sheep wool*)

Go to your father and tell him you're Esau. He'll feel your arms and think you're him. Then he'll bless you instead of Esau.

JACOB

Uh … all right. Thanks, Mom. Wait, but what about the soup?

REBEKAH

You'll think of something. Okay, go, go, go!
(*Rushes Jacob offstage; exits stage with Jacob*)

ISAAC

(*Enters stage slowly*)

Oh, how the years have caught up to me. I'm so old I can barely see. I pray my son Esau makes it on time ... Why on earth am I speaking in rhymes?

JACOB
(*From offstage*)
Father, are you there?

ISAAC
Yes. Who goes there?

JACOB
(*Enters stage*)
'Tis I, your eldest son, Esau.

ISAAC
Oh, really? Come near and let me hold thine arms.

JACOB
(*Walks to Isaac and holds out arm covered in sheep wool*)

ISAAC
(*Touches Jacob's arm*)
I hear Jacob, but I feel Esau. If you truly are Esau, then where is the soup I asked for?

JACOB
Uh ... Oh, Father, you already ate the soup. Don't you remember?
(*Closes eyes and crosses fingers*)

ISAAC
Huh? Oh, yes, of course! I must have forgotten. My memory must be fading away as well.

JACOB

(*Wipes head*)

Phew, that was close.

ISAAC

I'm sorry—what was that?

JACOB

Uh ... I said, bless me the most!

ISAAC

Yes, yes, I haven't forgotten my promise to you. Bow your head and I will bless thee.

JACOB

(*Bows head*)

ISAAC

(*Places hand on head*)

Now you are blessed.

ESAU

(*Enters stage with bowl*)

Father, I have the soup you asked—

(*Drops bowl*)

What is this madness?

JACOB

(*Sees Esau and exits stage*)

ESAU

(*Chases Jacob until he's offstage*)

Drat! He's offstage; I can't get him now!

ISAAC
Esau, what happened?

ESAU
That ankle-grabbing, birthright-stealing brother of mine just tricked you into blessing him instead of me. Can you still pray for me, Father?

ISAAC
Yes, but your brother ran off with your blessing …

ESAU
(*Yells to the sky*)
Curse you, Jacob!

ISAAC and ESAU
(*Begin to walk offstage*)

ISAAC
Well, let's look on the bright side. At least I didn't die this time.
(*Exits stage*)

FRONT MAN
Then Isaac died of old age.

ESAU
Spoke too soon.

FRONT MAN
(*Continues reading*)
This of course happened after Jacob was told to take a wife from Padan-aram instead of Canaan. And Jacob went out from Beersheba, and went toward Haran.

JACOB

(*Enters stage with stone and yawns*)

I'm so tired! I guess a little nap wouldn't hurt.

(*Places stone on ground and rests head on stone and tries to make himself comfortable; looks to audience*)

I don't know how he did it.

(*Rests on stone again*)

ANGEL

(*Enters stage and approaches Jacob with small ladder*)

JACOB

(*Awakens*)

Who are you supposed to be?

(*Raises fists*)

ANGEL

(*Shakes head*)

JACOB

We're not there yet? Oh, sorry.

(*Lowers fists*)

ANGEL

(*Climbs small ladder and points to the sky*)

THUNDERING VOICE

I lead your father and his father before him.

JACOB

I guess that makes you my leader too.

THUNDERING VOICE

Yup. Pretty much.

ANGEL and JACOB
>   (*Exit stage*)

FRONT MAN
>   (*Continues reading*)

Then Jacob awoke from the dream and vowed to serve God. Then he got married to a fair woman named Rachel—

CREWMAN #8
>   (*From offstage*)

Did someone say …
>   (*Enters stage*)
>   … Rachel?

CREWMAN #5
>   (*Enters stage*)

Psh! You already played Rebekah! You can't play Jacob's Mom and wife!

FRONT MAN

Yeah I'd rather we stay away from the whole Oedipal complex.

CREWMAN #7
>   (*Enters stage*)

You're right. After all, I think I'd be the best to play Rachel. You two can play Leah. You know? The ugly sister.
>   (*Looks at nails mockingly*)

CREWMAN #8

Oh no she didn't!
>   (*Rushes to CREWMAN #7, about to hit him*)

FRONT MAN and CREWMAN #5
   (*Stop* CREWMAN *#8*)

CREWMAN #5
   (*Goes over to* CREWMAN *#7 and whispers in his ear*)

CREWMAN #8
All I know is that I'd better play Joseph in the next scene! I mean, I barely have any stage time!

FRONT MAN
I already cast Joseph.

CREWMAN #3
   (*Enters stage*)
You called?

CREWMAN #8
   (*With attitude*)
Oh, I see. I didn't know this was a predominantly male cast!
   (*Exits stage*)

CREWMAN #2, #4, and #6
   (*From offstage*)
Boys rule!

CREWMAN #7
Oh, I didn't know Rachel steals from her father and dies.
   (*To* CREWMAN *#5*)
Today's your lucky day!
   (*Exits stage*)

CREWMAN #5
Guess I'm Rachel now.

(*Smiles to audience*)

Nah, just kidding. I need to get ready for act two … We're still doing that, right?

(*Slowly exits stage*)

FRONT MAN

Aw man, who's going to play Rachel now?

CREWMAN #3

(*Puts hand on Ffont man's shoulder*)

If I must …

FRONT MAN

No! No! No! It's okay. We'll just skip to Joseph's story.

CREWMAN #3

Oh, thank heavens!

(*Quickly exits stage*)

JACOB

(*Enters stage*)

Wait, but what about the wrestling scene? These people paid to see quality entertainment, and I will not disappoint.

FRONT MAN

Fine! Fine! Do the wrestling scene.

(*Exits stage*)

JACOB

Yes.

(*To audience*)

Wait right here

(*Exits stage*)

JACOB and ANGEL

> (*Enter with boxing gloves on; stand on opposing sides*)

CREWMAN #6

> (Enters center stage with microphone)

> (*Execute wrestling scene, CREWMAN #6 is the announcer, CREWMAN #5 is the "the girl holding signs with the match number on them" CREWMAN #4 is the angel's masseuse, CREWMAN #8 is Jacob's water boy*)

> (*Quick matches, three rounds, and on third round, angel hits Jacob's hip and wins*)

> (*All except for CREWMAN #6 exit after third round*)

ACT 1, SCENE 8

Joseph, not Lowseph

CREWMAN #6
(*Reads script*)
It seems as though we're running out of time! If you'd like to find out what happened next… just open the Bible! Genesis thirty-two, that is. Now on to Joseph's story. Joseph's father, Jacob, who now goes by the name Israel, had twelve sons, but that didn't matter because Jacob loved Joseph the most! We've already had two sibling scenes, neither of which ended well.
(*Mockingly*)
So guess what happened this time … But unlike his brothers, Joseph was a very special child. He had dreams that told the future.

JOSEPH
(*Enters stage*)
Yes I did!

CREWMAN #6
Wait you're not Joseph.

CREWMAN #3
(*Enters mumbling from side of stage with mouth taped and rope tied around him*)

CREWMAN #6
(*Looks offstage*)

What's going on back there?

JOSEPH
(*Rushes to* CREWMAN #3)
Oh, nothing. Nothing at all.
(*Pushes* CREWMAN #3 *back offstage*)
I think it's about time my brothers showed up!
(*Pulls* CREWMAN #2, #4, *and* #7 *onto stage*)

CREWMAN #2
What are you doing?

CREWMAN #7
This isn't in the script!

CREWMAN #4
Don't kill me!

JOSEPH
My brothers, I had a dream where we were binding sheaves in the field, and lo my sheaf arose and yours fell.

CREWMAN #2
What are you talking about?

JOSEPH
Don't get it? Okay, how about this: I had another dream where the sun, moon, and…
(*Counts all the crewmen onstage*)
Four stars made obeisance to me.

CREWMAN #4
What?

JOSEPH
Still nothing? Okay, how about this? I dreamt that the audience would adore my performance more than any of yours!

CREWMAN #7
Oh no you didn't!
(*Rushes to Joseph*)

CREWMEN #2 AND #4
(*Stop CREWMAN #7*)

CREWMAN #2
I have a better idea.
(*Brings them in for a huddle*)

CREWMAN #4 AND #7
Okay.
(*Exit stage*)

CREWMAN #2
(*Approaches and picks up Joseph*)

JOSEPH
What are you doing? Put me down.

CREWMEN #4 AND #7
(*Enter stage with the well*)

JOSEPH
No, not the well!

CREWMAN #2
(*Puts Joseph in the well*)

JOSEPH
Noooooooooooooo!
   (*Thud*)

CREWMAN #2
Well, well, well. That's it for Joseph ... or should I say *Lowseph*?
   (Laughs)

CREWMAN #6
How are you guys going to end this scene without him?

CREWMAN #7
Don't worry. We have an idea.

CREWMAN #6
   (*Exits stage*)

CREWMAN #2, #4, #7
   (*Snap fingers and harmonize*)

Joseph Triplet

D D-D C-C B-B A-A
Ba, Do-Ba, Do-Ba, Do-Ba, Do-Ba
1: G-G E-E A-A-A D-D E-F#
2: D-C B-A F-F-F A-A B-C#
3: D D D E
Do-Ba, Do-Ba, Do-ba-di, Do-Ba, Do-BaDo, Do, Do-Do
   (*Repeat through whole song*)
D-D G G G E-E E A-A A D-D
Lem-me tell you a sto-ry 'bout Jo-seph the dream-er-
D D-G G G E-E E A A A A#-B-D
Was be-trayed by his bro-thers but blessed by the re-deem-er-

D D G G G G-E-E E E A A A D
He was sold to the E-gyp-tians for the price of a pail

D D G G -G G E-E-E E E A-A A G D
He was lied a-bout by Pot-i-phar's wife and end-ed up in jail
G G G G E E A A A D
There he made some friends and soon he was free
D E G-G G G E E E A A A-A#-B-D
He told Phar-aoh 'bout his dreams and they lived in har-mo-ny-y
D G G G G E-E E E A G D
His bro-thers came to E-gypt and they knew him not
D G G G G E E E E A-A A D
They thought he was a dead man and his bo-dy had rot
G G-G E-E E E A A A-D
After Jo-seph tes-ted them he wept with re-joice
D D G G G G E-E E E A A G D
He was glad to hear his fam-ly not by name, but by voice
D E G-G G E-E-E E A A A D
He had Eph-raim and Ma-na-sseh, the sons to his wife.
D-D G G G A B-D B D E D B G
Ja-cob blessed them, and they were hap-py for the rest of their lives.
　　(*All exit stage*)

Front man
　　(*Enters stage*)
And thus concludes act one of two. We're going to have a short intermission so we can get this act together … hopefully. For now you can go [insert direction here] for food and refreshments.

Fin

ACT 2, SCENE 1

Exodus Stage Right

CREWMAN #8
(*Enters stage with a bag of popcorn*)
Oh, you came back?
(*Slowly starts exiting stage without looking away from audience*)
Well, um, to be honest, we weren't expecting you to come back.
(*Exits stage*)

CREWMAN #7
(*From offstage*)
What are you doing back here?

CREWMAN #8
(*From offstage*)
They're back!

CREWMAN #5
(*From offstage*)
Who's back?

CREWMAN #8
(From offstage)
The audience!

CREWMAN #7
(*From offstage, sarcastically*)

Gasp! You mean the ones that paid to be here?

CREWMAN #8
(*From offstage*)
Yeah, they came back. This wouldn't have happened if you didn't mention act two earlier.

CREWMAN #5
(*From offstage*)
When did I do that?

CREWMAN #8
(*From offstage*)
Act one, scene seven, page fifty-three!

CREWMAN #5
(*From offstage*)
Whoa, whoa, don't blame me! It was in the script.

CREWMAN #7
(*From offstage*)
Um, I don't think that's the page number. Speaking of pages, we've been rambling on for about two of them. Unless this is your idea of stalling, I suggest we get this show on the road before the boss comes in.

CREWMAN #5
(*From offstage*)
Good idea!
(*Enters stage*)
Hey, everyone! How are you? Good, good.
(*Exits stage frantically*)

CREWMAN #7
(*From offstage*)
Now what?

CREWMAN #5
(*From offstage*)
Uh. What are we doing again?

CREWMAN #8
(*From offstage*)
Act two, scene one!

CREWMAN #5
(*From offstage*)
Oh, right!

CREWMAN #7
(*From offstage*)
The clock is ticking! These people came to see quality entertainment. I will not go down as the one who just sat by while my crew members choked.

CREWMAN #8
(*From offstage*)
What are you doing?

CREWMAN #7
(*From offstage*)
I'm going in.
(*Enters stage*)
All right, look. The crew and I have been working our tails off to provide you with retelling of the first two books of the Bible in a rather ... humorous way. We fell a bit behind schedule and—

CREWMEN #5 AND #8
  (*Enter stage*)
Don't tell them that!
  (*Exit stage while pulling* CREWMAN #7 *offstage*)

CREWMAN #7
  (*From offstage*)
Now what?

CREWMAN #8
  (*From offstage*)
If you say something like that, then people will want their money back.

CREWMAN #7
  (*From offstage*)
Oh, no, no, no. No refunds! I'm sure the ticket person made that loud and clear.

CREWMAN #5
  (*From offstage*)
Okay, ladies, you know what our problem is? We've gotta have faith! Maybe it's the nerves from completing act one. Whatever it is, though, we can't let it interfere with our faith.

CREWMAN #7
  (*From offstage*)
  You're right.

CREWMAN #8
  (*From offstage*)
Lord forgive us.

FRONT MAN

(*Enters stage from a different entrance*)

CREWMAN #5

(*From offstage*)

Now, let's go out there and claim our rightful place in the history books as the greatest crewmen the world has ever seen!

(*Enters stage and is shocked to see* FRONT MAN)

CREWMAN #7 AND #8

(*From offstage*)

Yeah!

(*Enters stage and is shocked to see* FRONT MAN)

FRONT MAN

What's the holdup?

CREWMAN #5 AND #7

(*Exit stage quickly*)

CREWMAN #8

Oh, hey, boss! Um, we had a bit of trouble getting back onstage. We felt kind of worried. I guess you could say …

(*Starts chuckling*)

… we couldn't find our … Exodus!

(*Exits stage laughing*)

FRONT MAN

I won't even go into detail about how … Wait. Exodus? I know what that is!

ACT 2, SCENE 2

Water Boy

FRONT MAN
After Jacob and his family died—don't worry; they lived a good life before that happened—the Egyptians caught wind of the Israelites growing in numbers, so the new Pharaoh decided to put them in bondage.

PHARAOH
That's enough! I shall take it from here.

FRONT MAN
Um … excuse me?

PHARAOH
'Tis I! Pharaoh the …
(*Counts fingers*)
… third ruler of Egypt. I'll take it from here.

FRONT MAN
Hey, you're making my job a lot easier.
(*Exits stage with ease*)

PHARAOH
(*Hands to mouth*)
All muh Hebrew ladies!

SHIPHRAH and PUAH
> (*Enter stage in handcuffs*)

PHARAOH
Modern handcuffs? A little ahead of our time here, don't you think?

SHIPHRAH
You called, Pharaoh?

PHARAOH
Yes, yes I did. Shiphrah, Puah, I gave you two a job, didn't I? I specifically remembered telling you two to kill the child of the mother in labour if it is a boy and spare the child if it is a girl.

PUAH
Yes, Pharaoh, we remembered.

PHARAOH
Then why are the Hebrew boys still alive?

SHIPHRAH
Hold that thought!
> (*Turns around with Puah*)
I told you he'd notice.

PUAH
Oh, don't pin this on me. I remember specifically telling you to hide them.

SHIPHRAH
Hide them? Hide them! With what, exactly? Some fresh fine-twined linen?

PHARAOH

I've waited long enough! Guard!

GUARD

(*Enters stage with a leather jacket and sunglasses*)

Eh, Pharaoh. Whaddya need?

PHARAOH

W-what is this? Never mind. Get these two women out of here. While you're at it, tell the other guards—preferably the ones from this time period—that every son that is born ye shall cast into the river and every daughter ye shall save alive.

(*Exits stage*)

GUARD

Ha, this guy. No problem, boss man.

(*Escorts Shiphrah and Puah offstage*)

SHIPHRAH

You'll never get away with this, Pharaoh!

PUAH

We Hebrew women are not as the Egyptian women, for they are lively and are delivered ere the midwives come in unto them.

(*Exits stage with guard and Shiphrah*)

FRONT MAN

(*Enters stage and begins reading*)

And there went a man of the house of Levi, and took to wife a daughter of Levi. And the woman conceived, and bare a son … Guess who this is. She hid him for three months before having to put him in an ark of bulrushes, and daubed it with slime and with pitch …

CREWMAN #4
  (*Enters stage pulling ark onto stage*)

FRONT MAN
What are you doing?

CREWMAN #4
I thought you said she had to put him in an ark. Here's the ark.

FRONT MAN
Not that kind of ark. Put that back and wait for your cue.

CREWMAN #4
  (*Sighs and exits stage with the ark*)

FRONT MAN
Where was I?
  (*Continues reading*)
And daubed it with slime and with pitch, and put the child therein; and she laid it in the flags by the river's brink.

JOCHEBED
  (*Enters stage with baby basket*)
Miriam, please watch your baby brother, Moses, as I put him in the water. Be sure that no harm comes of him.

MIRIAM
  (*Enters stage rushing beside Jochebed*)
Yes, Jochebed, I will.

JOCHEBED
  (*With sass*)
Mm. What did you just call me?

MIRIAM

Mom. I meant Mom. My mistake.

JOCHEBED

All right. Just don't let that happen again.
(*Puts baby basket center stage and exits stage*)

MIRIAM

(*Hides in corner and slowly falls asleep*)

PHAROAH'S DAUGHTER

(*Enters stage*)
Oh, what a long day. I'm so worn out after all of that hard work I watched my dad's guards do. I think I need bath.
(*Looks at* FRONT MAN *with a cautious face*)

FRONT MAN

What?

PHAROAH'S DAUGHTER

I can't do it while you're looking! Turn around.
(*Notices the baby basket*)
Gasp! What is that?
(*Claps twice*)
Maid! Go fetch it for me.
(*Looks around*)
Maid … maid?

MAID

(*Enters stage with a leather jacket and sunglasses*)
Eh! Pharaoh's daughter. Whaddya need?

PHAROAH'S DAUGHTER
You're not my maid! You're a … a joke.

MAID
No. You want a joke? What's your name? Huh? Huh? That's right …
You ain't got a name.

PHAROAH'S DAUGHTER
(*Walks toward the maid angrily*)
I'll have you know that I most certainly—

FRONT MAN
Sorry to interrupt, but we've got this play going on …

PHAROAH'S DAUGHTER
Oh! Right. Maid, fetch me that thing in the water over there.

MAID
You mean the thing right in front of us? The thing you could easily
grab yourself?

PHAROAH'S DAUGHTER
Ah, ah, ah. No questions.
(*Points at baby basket whilst looking away*)

MAID
(*Fetches baby basket and gives it to Pharaoh's daughter*)
That thing's pretty heavy. What do you think is in it?

PHAROAH'S DAUGHTER
One way to find out.
(*Opens the baby basket*)
Gasp! This is one of the Hebrews' children.

MAID

D-did you just say *gasp*? I think you were literally supposed to ... Whatever. Shall I go and call to thee a nurse of the Hebrew women, that she may nurse the child for thee?

PHARAOH'S DAUGHTER

Go.

MAID

(*Hands to mouth*)
All muh Hebrew ladies!

JOCHEBED

(*Enters stage*)
Yes?

PHARAOH'S DAUGHTER

Take this child I found in the water, that you have obviously never met in your life. Take this child away and nurse it for me, and I will give thee thy wages.

JOCHEBED

If you say so. After I nurse him what will you name him?

PHARAOH'S DAUGHTER

Well ... since I found him in the water ... I'll name him ...

JOCHEBED

Mo ... ssssssss

PHARAOH'S DAUGHTER

Water boy ... No, that doesn't sound very threatening. "Then water boy said, Let my people go" doesn't sound as cool as ...

JOCHEBED
Mmmo

PHARAOH'S DAUGHTER
Moses! That's a perfect name! I'll name him Moses.
 (*Exits stage*)

JOCHEBED
Oh, praise the Lord.
 (*Exits stage with baby basket*)

MAID
 (*Walks over to Miriam*)
Um, excuse me?

MIRIAM
 (*Wakes up from sleep*)
Huh, yeah, what?

MAID
The exit is this way.
 (*Exits stage*)

MIRIAM
Oh, right.
 (*Exits stage*)

FRONT MAN
 (*Continues reading*)
And it came to pass in those days, when Moses was grown, that he went out unto his brethren, and looked on their burdens: and he spied an Egyptian smiting a Hebrew, one of his brethren.

PRISONER 1
(Enters stage with handcuffs on)

GUARD
(Enters stage with a whip)
Eh, prisoner, I'm gonna beat you.
(Whips the prisoner)

MOSES
(Enters stage dramatically)
Let my people go!

FRONT MAN
Um ... not yet.

MOSES
Not yet?
(Looks at the prisoner and the guard)
Oh!
(Puts the guard into a sleeper hold)

GUARD
(Dramatically falls asleep)

PRISONER 1
(Gasps)
Did you just ...?

MOSES
(Drags the guard's body offstage while looking at the prisoner with rage)
Shh ... You. Saw. Nothing. Nothing!
(Exits stage with the guard)

PRISONER 2

(Enters stage in handcuffs and begins fighting with PRISONER 1)

MOSES

(Enters stage)

What is this? Preposterous! I return at the wake of the day to be greeted by this atrocious sight? Hebrew brethren thou art and yet you stand here to fight? Why smites thou thy fellow?

PRISONERS 1 AND 2

(Both stop fighting to look at Moses awkwardly)

PRISONER 2

(Looks at PRISONER 1)

I got this.

PRISONER 1

You sure?

PRISONER 2

Yeah ... I speak English. Who made thee a prince and a judge over us? Intendest thou to kill me, as thou killedest the Egyptian?

MOSES

(Angrily looks at PRISONER 1)

You little rat! What did I tell you? You saw nothing!

(Aggressively walks towards PRISONER 1)

PRISONER 1 AND 2

(Exit stage, from offstage)

Pharaoh, Pharaoh, Moses killed an Egyptian!

PHARAOH

(From offstage)

What! Send everyone—all my men, the lancers, the archers, the swordsmen, the shield men, the gunmen! Fire all the weapons at once!

MOSES
(*In panic runs in spot*)
I gotta get outta here!I know! I'll escape to Midian and hide there.
(*Exits stage*)

FRONT MAN
(*Continues reading*)
Now the priest of Midian had seven daughters: and they came and drew water, and filled the troughs to water their father's flock.

REUEL
(*Enters stage*)
I, Reuel, the priest of Midian, have seven daughters. They draw water for my flock and—

FRONT MAN
I already said all of that.

REUEL
Good. Let's skip the formalities and get to the good part. Daughters, daughters, big and small, Who's the best Midian priest of them all?

ZIPPORAH
(*Enters stage and rolls eyes*)
This again, Daddy?

REUEL
Whoa, you got here really fast.

ZIPPORAH

(*Flustered*)

Well … this Egyptian delivered us out of the hand of the shepherds, and also drew water enough for us, and watered the flock.

REUEL

Was this Egyptian a boy?

ZIPPORAH

(*Giggles*)

Well, gee, I, well, ha, you know, I … Yes, Daddy, he is.

REUEL

And where is he? Why is it that ye have left the man? Call him, that he may eat bread.

ZIPPORAH

(*Puts both hands over mouth*)

Oh, water boy!

MOSES

(*Enters stage*)

You called?

ZIPPORAH

Meet my daddy.

MOSES

Whoa, whoa. I barely know you and now you want me to meet your father? I was hoping we could take things slowly.

ZIPPORAH

(*Flirtatiously*)

We can take things as slowly as you want after the marriage.

(*Exits stage slowly*)

REUEL

(*Steps between their line of view*)

Yeah, water boy, after the marriage! My daughter is yours. Stay with us here in Midian. You've got nothing to lose.

MOSES

You're right! I have absolutely nothing to lose. Nothing could make me want to leave this place. I have everything I could need right here. Yup, life is good.

FRONT MAN

(*Continues reading*)

After Zipporah had a son named Gershom with Moses, the king of Egypt died, the Israelites cried because they were still in captivity, and God, hearing their groaning, remembered the covenant he made with his chosen people.

Bushco Inferno

JETHRO
All right, water boy. I need you to keep my flock and lead them to the
back side of the desert.

MOSES
Uh, Reuel. My name is Moses.

JETHRO
Uh, Moses. My name is Jethro.

MOSES
Huh? But …
    (*Looks at* FRONT MAN)
You said—

FRONT MAN
Hey, don't look at me! His name just changes. I think one's just a
nickname or something.

MOSES
Kind of like Simon Peter?

JETHRO
Who?

MOSES
Never mind. I'll do what you said earlier with the sheep and stuff.

JETHRO
And I'll watch from a distance. A really, really far distance.
    (*Exits stage*)

MOSES
    (*Steps forward*)
Look, a burning—

FRONT MAN
Wait for it!

CREWMAN #4
    (*Enters stage with burning bush*)
Do I really have to do this?

FRONT MAN
Just be thankful you're still alive in this scene.

CREWMAN #4
    (*Exits stage*)

MOSES
Look, a burning bush!

BUSH
Moses, Moses.

MOSES
Look, a talking bush.

BUSH

Draw not nigh hither: put off thy shoes from off thy feet, for the place whereon thou standest is holy ground.

MOSES

(*Takes off his shoes*)

Who are you?

BUSH

The one who leads Abraham, Isaac, and Jacob.

MOSES

(*Hides in corner*)

BUSH

I have surely seen the affliction of my people who are in Egypt and have heard their cry by reason of their taskmasters; for I know their sorrows—

MOSES

Wait, wait, wait. The one who led Abraham, Isaac, and Jacob? You have a job for me, don't you …?

BUSH

And I am come down to deliver them out of the hand of the Egyptians, and to bring them up out of that land unto a good land and a large, unto a land flowing with milk and honey—

MOSES

So you want me to go into Egypt and bring the Israelites out? I don't know if I can do that.

BUSH

Let me finish! I will be with thee. And if they ask who it is that sent you, you will respond—

MOSES

(*Gets out of corner*)

Let my people go! Right?

BUSH

You will respond, I AM THAT I AM ... Thus shalt thou say unto the children of Israel, I AM hath sent me unto you.

MOSES

But what if they don't believe me?

BUSH

You're talking to a burning bush! You really think ... Okay, look, what is that in your hand?

MOSES

(*Looks in his hand*)

The rod that I carried with me from watching the sheep?

BUSH

Yes. Throw it on the ground.

MOSES

(*Throws the rod on the ground*)

THE SERPENT

(*Enters stage and rushes to the ground where Moses' staff is*)

Sssssss!

MOSES
Gasp!

BUSH
Need I say more? Now, just remember, when the people of Israel are freed, tell them to come to Mount Horeb to worship God.

MOSES
But I'm not that good at speaking.

BUSH
You said that sentence perfectly fine … but if you insist, bring your brother Aaron and—

MOSES
Aaron is my brother? What!

BUSH
Yes, and he's good at speaking too. He'll approach you when you get to Egypt.

MOSES
Okay, I'll go right away.
   (*Begins to run offstage*)

BUSH
Aren't you forgetting something?

THE SERPENT
Sssssss

MOSES
Oh yeah.
   (*Goes to pick up*)

THE SERPENT

Whoa, whoa. I'll leave myself.

>*(Exits stage with burning bush)*

MOSES

>*(Exits stage with the rod)*

Act 2, Scene 4: Plague Palace

PHARAOH

>*(Enters stage pacing)*

GUARD

>*(Enters stage standing at attention)*

FRONT MAN

>*(Continues reading)*

After Moses went to Egypt with his wife and children, whom later cause quite an argument, he found Aaron, got him caught up with what was going on, and had him speak to the people of Israel. They bowed their heads and worshipped once they knew the words came from the true and living God. But not all was solved yet. He still had to confront the new Pharaoh. Exodus five, if you're curious.

PHARAOH

Guard, make sure no one gets in my palace. I've been thinking heavy thoughts, and my heart feels as if it's frozen solid.

GUARD

You got it, boss.

AARON

>*(Enters stage)*

You mean you put your hand in your bosom and it came out grotesque?

MOSES

(*Enters stage*)

Yeah! Leprous even. Then God told me to take water from the river and pour it on dry land, and that it would turn into blood. He practically gave me powers to prove these things to Pharaoh.

PHARAOH

(*Looks at Moses and Aaron, turns to guard*)

Guard! What did I just say?

GUARD

(*Exits stage covering face in shame*)

PHARAOH

So … you must be this Moses I've heard about. Any last words before I—

MOSES

(*Points at Pharaoh*)

Let my people go!

PHARAOH

What?

AARON

I'll take it from here, Moses.

(*Puts arm around Pharaoh*)

Pharaoh, buddy, king, guy… You're an aspiring dictator, right? Well, what my brother Moses here is trying to say is, we can't have someone as … young, ambitious, and overbearing as you leading over the people of God. I mean, the old Pharaoh died, and you've got to admit that the comparisons between you two are warranted. I mean, you guys practically look alike. But do you want to be remembered as the Pharaoh that kept God's people prisoner?

(*Lets go of Pharaoh and walks back to Moses*)

I think not.

PHARAOH

Bah! Who is the LORD, that I should obey his voice to let Israel go? I know not the LORD, neither will I let Israel go. Instead I will make their labour twice as hard! Ha-ha-ha! Instead of being given straw to make bricks with clay … they will have to find the straw themselves.

MOSES and AARON

(*Walk to opposite side of the stage from Pharaoh*)

FRONT MAN

(*Continues reading*)

Pharaoh was cruel. The people were angry with Moses for even talking to Pharaoh. Moses began to question why God chose him to do this task, only for more evil to fall on his people. Moses didn't quite understand that God had a divine plan. God reassured Moses that indeed Pharaoh would let God's people go to the Promised Land flowing with milk and honey. The next morning …

MOSES and AARON

(*Walk towards Pharaoh*)

MOSES

Let my people go!

PHARAOH

This again? Guard, where are you?

GUARD
>(*From offstage*)
>
Nope, sorry. Can't hear you.

MOSES
>(*Gives Aaron his rod*)

THE SERPENT
(Enters stage quietly)

AARON
Fine, try doubting God's power after this.
>(*Throws rod down*)

THE SERPENT
>(*Simultaneously jumps to the ground*)
>
Sssssss!

PHARAOH
>(*Frightened*)
>
Oh my ... what? Ha, you think that's special? Psh ... I ... uh ... my men can do that too.
>(*Puts hands to mouth*)
>
All my magic makers!

SORCERER
>(*Enters stage melodramatically with toy snake up sleeves*)
>
Brother Magician!

MAGICIAN
>(*Enters stage melodramatically with toy snake up sleeve*)
>
Yes, Brother?

SORCERER
How are you?

MAGICIAN
Fine, thank you. Brother Enchanter!

ENCHANTER
(*Enters stage melodramatically with toy snake up sleeve*)
Yes, Brother?

MAGICIAN
How are you?

ENCHANTER
Fine, thank you. Brother Sorcerer, how are you?

SORCERER
Juuuuuuuuuust … peachy!

PHARAOH
(*Stands up straight*)
All of you show these men the power of the greatest magic of all …
money!

MAGICIAN, ENCHANTER, and SORCERER
(*Throw down their snakes*)
Presto!

AARON
Whoa … now what?

MOSES
(*Puts a finger to his own mouth*)
Shh! Look.

(*Points at the serpent*)

THE SERPENT
(*Dramatically eats the other snakes*)
Sssssss!
(*Stands up and looks directly at the magician, enchanter, and sorcerer*)

MAGICIAN, ENCHANTER, and SORCERER
(*Exit stage tripping over each other in a hurry*)

THE SERPENT
Yeah, that's what I thought
(*Looks at Pharaoh*)
Sssssss!

PHARAOH
What? You think I'm afraid? I'm still not letting them go.

MOSES
Then I will … Wait a minute.
(*Whispers into Aaron's ear and steps to opposite side of stage from Pharaoh*)

AARON
Then we will strike the water with his rod and it will turn into blood. And the fish that is in the river shall die, and the river shall stink; and the Egyptians shall loathe to drink the water of the river.
(*Steps to opposite side of stage from Pharaoh*)

FRONT MAN
(*Continues reading*)

And then what they said would happen happened the next morning. A week passed, and God sent Moses and Aaron to ... well, just watch.

MOSES
(*Walks towards Pharaoh*)
Let my people go!

PHARAOH
(*Falls to knees*)
Oh, thank goodness you're here.

AARON
(*Walks towards Pharaoh*)
What's the deal, Pharaoh?

PHARAOH
Everything you said happened.

MOSES and AARON
(*High-five without looking at each other*)

PHARAOH
Please get rid of the blood and I'll free your people.

AARON
Should we trust him, Moses?

MOSES
Aaron, Pharaoh might be a bad guy, but even he has a heart.

AARON
Let's just hope it's not a hard one.

MOSES
(*Whispers into Aaron's ear*)

AARON
If you don't let God's people go, a plague of frogs will fall upon Egypt.

MOSES
Yeah, frogs!

MOSES and AARON
(*Walk to opposite side of stage from Pharaoh*)

FRONT MAN
(*Continues reading*)
But Pharaoh didn't keep his word.

PHARAOH
(*To audience*)
I had my fingers crossed.

FRONT MAN
(*Continues reading*)
So the frogs came. Enter frogs!

CREWMAN #7
(*Enters stage and places frog on Pharaoh's head; proceeds to exit stage*)

FRONT MAN
(*Continues reading*)
The next week God sent Moses and Aaron again.

MOSES
(*Walks over to Pharaoh*)

Let my people go!

PHARAOH
Or what?

AARON
(*Walks over to Pharaoh*)
Gnats!

PHARAOH
Bring it on!

CREWMEN #5, #7, and #8
(*Enter stage with gnats and throw them at Pharaoh; proceed to exit stage*)

FRONT MAN
On the fourth week …

MOSES
Let my people go!

PHARAOH
Or what?

AARON
Flies!

PHARAOH
Psh, is that all?

CREWMEN #5, #7, and #8
(*Enter stage with flies and throw them at Pharaoh; proceed to exit stage*)

FRONT MAN
On the fifth week ...

MOSES
Let my people go!

PHARAOH
Or what?

AARON
Disease!

PHARAOH
Uh ... that sounds kind of bad!

CREWMEN #5, #7, and #8
   (*Enter stage with black markers and draw on Pharaoh; proceed to exit stage*)

FRONT MAN
On the sixth week ...

MOSES
Let my people go!

PHARAOH
Or what?

AARON
Boils!

PHARAOH
But ... isn't that a disease!

CREWMEN #5, #7, AND #8
(Enter stage with red markers and draw on Pharaoh)
Nope!
(Proceeds to exit stage)

FRONT MAN
On the seventh week …

MOSES
Let my people go!

PHARAOH
Or what?

AARON
Hail!

PHARAOH
In Egypt?

CREWMAN #5, #7, AND #8
(Enter stage with Ping-Pong balls and throw them at Pharaoh, proceed to exit stage)

FRONT MAN
On the eighth week …

MOSES
Let my people go!

PHARAOH
Or what?

AARON
Locusts!

PHARAOH
But we already had flies and gnats!

CREWMEN #5, #7, AND #8
(*Enter stage with locusts and throw them at Pharaoh, proceed to exit stage*)

FRONT MAN
On the ninth week …

MOSES
Let my people go!

PHARAOH
Or what?

AARON
Darkness!

PHARAOH
Ha! And how do you plan on doing that?

CREWMEN #5, #7, AND #8
(*Enter stage with big black blanket and wrap it around Pharaoh, proceed to exit stage*)

FRONT MAN
On the tenth week …

MOSES
Let my people go!

PHARAOH
Or what?

AARON
Death!

PHARAOH
You plan on killing me?

AARON
Not your death, Pharaoh! All the firstborn in the land of Egypt shall die, from the firstborn of Pharaoh that sitteth upon his throne, even unto the firstborn of the maidservant that is behind the mill; and all the firstborn of beasts. And there shall be a great cry throughout all the land of Egypt such as there was none like it, nor shall be like it any more.

PHARAOH
Whoa … that sounds pretty vicious.

AARON
Will you let God's people go?

PHARAOH
No. I don't believe you.

MOSES and AARON
(*Exit stage*)

FRONT MAN
(*Continues reading*)
Moses and Aaron went to the people of Israel and told them that after the tenth and final plague, Pharaoh would have no choice but to let them go. But Moses gave them a special order: he told them that God

would send down his angel to the houses in Egypt. Moses said that the head of the Israelite families must take the blood of a year-old lamb and put it across the top of the door and on the doorstep. That way, the angel would know not to tamper with that house. He also instructed them to roast the meat of the lamb, eat it while standing by the table with the family, and throw any leftovers into the fire. They called this Passover. He also made sure they would be dressed to leave Egypt when God gave them a sign. In the morning, Pharaoh demanded that the Israelites leave immediately so that God wouldn't bring any more harm to Egypt. But—

CREWMEN #5, #7, and #8
(*Scream from offstage*)

PHARAOH
(*Ears covered*)
Guard, where are Moses and the Israelites heading?

GUARD
(*Enters stage with ears covered*)
They went south-east toward Mount Horeb.

PHARAOH
What? Why?

GUARD
Y-you just told them to leave …

PHARAOH
Nonsense! After them! Send everyone! All my men, the lancers, the archers, the swordsmen, the shield men, the gunmen! Six hundred charioteers! Fire all the weapons at once! Kill them and bring them back alive!

(*Exits stage*)

GUARD

(*Looks at audience, pointing at Pharaoh*)

Can you believe this guy?

(*Exits stage*)

FRONT MAN

(*Continues reading*)

And the angel of God, which went before the camp of Israel, removed and went behind them; and the pillar of the cloud went from before their face, and stood behind them: And it came between the camp of the Egyptians and the camp of Israel; and it was a cloud and darkness to them, but it gave light by night to these: so that the one came not near the other all the night. Pharaoh's men chased after the Israelites all the way to the Red Sea. It was there that God showed his mighty power to the Israelites once again, even though they began to doubt him.

CREWMEN #2 AND #7

(*Enter stage and holds Red Sea in the air center stage*)

MOSES

(*Enters stage; raises his arms with rod in right hand*)

CREWMEN #2 AND #7

(*Separate the Red Sea; one holds up the cloud of light on Moses' side, and the other holds up cloud of darkness on Pharaoh's side*)

MOSES

(*Walks through the Red Sea and turns to face Pharaoh*)

PHARAOH

(*Enters stage*)

Moses!

MOSES
Let my people go!

PHARAOH
Never!
(*Rushes through the Red Sea*)

MOSES
(*Raises arms*)

CREWMEN #2 AND #7
(*Close the Red Sea, merging the clouds back to one with the cloud light covering the other cloud.*)

PHARAOH
Ah! You think this water will kill me? Think again! This isn't the end. Moses! This isn't—

CREWMEN #2 AND #7
(*Exit stage with Pharaoh*)

PHARAOH
Wait, I'm not done. I'm not!
(*Exits stage*)

MOSES
Phew, what an adventure. I will sing unto the LORD, for he hath triumphed gloriously: the horse and his rider hath he thrown into the sea. The LORD is my strength and song, and he is become my salvation: he is my God, and I will prepare him an habitation; my father's God, and I will exalt him. Exodus fifteen, Exodus fifteen, Exodus fifteen to read the rest.

FRONT MAN

Looks as if someone didn't remember his lines.

MOSES

Lines? What lines? The play is over now! Everyone, we can take a bow.

CREWMEN #2, #3, #4, #5, #6, #7, #8
(*Enter stage with sighs and comments of relief*)

FRONT MAN
(*Stands up*)
Guys, guys, guys! The play isn't over.

CREWMEN #1, #2, #3, #4, #5, #6, #7, #8

What!

FRONT MAN

In case you've forgotten, we're doing all of Exodus.

CREWMEN #4

But isn't this where Moses's story ends, right when the Egyptians are defeated by the Red Sea? That's always how it ends!

FRONT MAN

Maybe in movies. But this isn't a movie. This is a play. And in this play, we are going to do all of Exodus.

CREWMEN #1, #2, #3, #4, #5, #6, #7, #8
(*Exits stage with sighs of disappointment*)

FRONT MAN
Now, where were we?

ACT 2, SCENE 5

Wilderness Warriors

FRONT MAN

(*Continues reading*)

So Moses brought Israel from the Red Sea, and they went out into the wilderness of Shur; and they went three days in the wilderness, and found no water. And when they came to Marah, they could not drink of the waters of Marah, for they were bitter: therefore the name of it was called Marah.

MOSES

(*Enters stage*)

People of Israel, we must continue.

AARON

(*Enters stage*)

Moses is right. Let's go.

HUR

(*Enters stage, to audience*)

Hey everybody. I'm Hur. Don't worry, I'll be really important later.

ISRAELITE 1

(*Enters stage*)

We've been travelling together for so long. How could we forget?

ISRAELITE 2

(*Enters stage*)

We, the people of Israel, are thirsty. What shall we drink?

MOSES

The Lord showed me a tree. He said to put it into the water to make it sweet.

ISRAELITE 1

Well? Get on with it!

MOSES

(*Throws tree from pocket onto the ground*)

ISRAELITE 1 AND 2

(*Leap towards the ground and drink the water*)

MOSES

If thou wilt diligently hearken to the voice of the LORD thy God, and will do that which is right in his sight, and wilt give ear to his commandments, and keep all his statutes, I will put none of these diseases upon thee, which I have brought upon the Egyptians: for I am the LORD that healeth thee.

ISRAELITE 1

(*Drinking water without listening*)

Whatever you say, boss man.

FRONT MAN

On the fifteenth day of the second month ...

ISRAELITE 2

Ugh! Would to God we had died by the hand of the LORD in the land of Egypt, when we sat by the flesh pots, and when we did eat bread the full; for ye have brought us forth into this wilderness, to kill this whole assembly with hunger?

MOSES
Wow …

THUNDERING VOICE
Behold, I will rain bread from heaven for you; and the people shall go out and gather a certain rate every day, that I may prove them, whether they will walk in my law or no.

MOSES
Then ye shall know that the LORD hath brought you out from the land of Egypt …

AARON
And in the morning, then ye shall see the glory of the LORD; for that he heareth your murmurings against the LORD: and what are we, that ye murmur against us?

MOSES
This shall be, when the LORD shall give you in the evening flesh to eat, and in the morning bread to the full; for that the LORD heareth your murmuring which ye murmur against him: and what are we? Your murmurings are not against us, but against the LORD.

MOSES, AARON, HUR, and ISRAELITE 1 and 2
    (*Rest on the ground*)

FRONT MAN
    (*Continues reading*)
In the night, birds were caught and eaten for food, but then … in the morning came an even bigger surprise.

CREWMAN #7
(*Enters stage and sprinkles flakes of manna all around, places rock on the ground, and exits stage*)

MOSES
(*Wakes up and stands*)
Israelites, wake up!

AARON, HUR, AND ISRAELITE 1 AND 2
(*Wake up and stand*)

HUR
(*Looks at Moses*)
What is it, Moses?

MOSES
The Lord God almighty has given us a miracle! He has granted us favor and produced a delightful nutrient for us to carry on this long travel ahead. The Promised Land may be far, but God is with us now and he will continue to be forevermore. If the journey is where one finds themselves, then with God we shall find much more. To God be the glory!

AARON, HUR, and ISRAELITE 1 and 2
(*Give confused look*)

HUR
Um … what is it, Moses?

MOSES
Huh? Oh, manna. This will be called manna. Try some.

AARON, HUR, and ISRAELITE 1 and 2
(*Try some*)

MOSES
What's it like?

ISRAELITE 1
Coriander seed, white.

ISRAELITE 2
It tastes like wafers made with honey.

MOSES
White like milk, tastes like honey? Hmm. Where have I heard that
before?
    (*Smiles while looking upward*)
This is the thing which the LORD commandeth, Fill an omer of it to
be kept for your generations; that they may see the bread wherewith
I have fed you in the wilderness, when I brought you forth from the
land of Egypt. Including you, Aaron.

AARON
Okay.

FRONT MAN
    (*Continues reading*)
And the children of Israel did eat manna forty years, until they came
to a land inhabited; they did eat manna, until they came unto the
borders of the land of Canaan. Now an omer is the tenth part of an
ephah. And all the congregation of the children of Israel journeyed
from the wilderness of Sin, after their journeys, according to the
commandment of the LORD, and pitched in Rephidim: and there
was no water for the people to drink.

ISRAELITE 1
    (*Rushes over to Moses*)
Moses, we're thirsty! Give us water that we may drink.

MOSES
Wow ... Why chide with me? Wherefore do ye tempt the LORD?
(*Looks upward*)
What shall I do unto this people? They be almost ready to stone me.

THUNDERING VOICE
Behold, I will stand before thee there upon the rock in Horeb; and thou shalt smite the rock, and there shall come water out of it, that the people may drink.

MOSES
(*Strikes rock on the ground*)

ISRAELITE 1 AND 2
(*Rush to drink from the rock*)

HUR
(*Picks up rock after*)

MOSES
I will call this place Massah, and Meribah, because of the chiding of the children of Israel, and because they tempted the LORD, saying, Is the LORD among us, or not?

FRONT MAN
(*Continues reading*)
Then came the Amalek, and fought with Israel in Raphidim.

MOSES
Wait! We're going to war?

FRONT MAN
Yes, that's what it says.

MOSES
What else does it say?

FRONT MAN
And Moses said unto Joshua—

MOSES
(*Frantically*)
Which one of you guys is Joshua?

ISRAELITE 1
(*Spins around*)

JOSHUA
I am Joshua!

MOSES
(*Walks over to Joshua*)
Perfect. I have a message for you …
(*Moses looks at* FRONT MAN *and says*)
Well, go on.

FRONT MAN
(*Continues reading*)
And Moses said unto Joshua, Choose us out men, and go out, fight
with Amalek: tomorrow I will stand on the top of the hill with the
rod of God in mine hand.

MOSES
(*With arm on Joshua's shoulder*)
Choose us out men …
(*Points at* FRONT MAN)
Everything he said. I'm going to go up to the top of the hill. I need
two people to come with me.

AARON
I'm your guy.

HUR
Me too.

MOSES
Who are you?

HUR
I'm Hur, guys, remember? Hur?

MOSES
Ben-Hur?

HUR
No, I'm real. You guys don't remember Hur?

AARON
I know a she, but not a her.

MOSES
Enough. Let's go.

MOSES, AARON, and HUR
(Walk stage left)

MOSES
Here we are, the top of the hill.

AARON
And here come the Amalekites.

AMALEKITE 1
(Enters stage right)
We have come to conquer and kill!

AMALEKITE 2
(Enters stage right)
Starting with you! The Israelites!

JOSHUA
Why?

AMALEKITE 1 AND 2
Uh ...

AMALEKITE 1
(To Amalekite 2)
Why do we want to kill them?

AMALEKITE 2
I don't have a clue. I thought we were just going to.
(To Amalekite 1)

AMALEKITE 1
Just because?

AMALEKITE 2
For the laughs, maybe?

AMALEKITE 1
Yeah, good enough.
(To Joshua and Israelite 2)
We wage war against Israel, just for the laughs!

JOSHUA
Well then.
    (*Draws swords, gives one to Israelite 2, looks directly at audience*)
Let there be laughs!

JOSHUA and ISRAELITE 2
    (*Begin fighting with Amalekite 1 and 2*)

MOSES
    (*Raises hands*)

JOSHUA and ISRAELITE 2
    (*Winning the fight*)

MOSES
    (*Lowers hands*)

JOSHUA and ISRAELITE 2
    (*Losing the fight*)

MOSES
    (*Plays with this*)
It seems like every time I raise my hands, Israel starts winning. But every time I lower my hands, they start to lose.

HUR
Then just keep your hands up and we'll win.

MOSES
I would … but my hands are so heavy.

HUR
    (*Pulls out rock*)
Here, sit on this. Aaron, Hur, and I will hold your hands up for you.

MOSES
    (*Sits on the rock*)

AARON AND HUR
    (*Raise Moses's hands, one at each side*)

FRONT MAN
    (*Continues reading*)
And his hands were steady until the going down of the sun.

AMALEKITE 2
    (*Falls to the ground*)

JOSHUA
    (*Stabs Amalekite 1*)

AMALEKITE 1
Ah!
    (*Falls to the ground*)
What is your name, brave warrior?

JOSHUA
Joshua! Don't you ever forget it!

AMALEKITE 1
    (*Stands up and exits stage with Amalekite 2 in arms*)

MOSES
    (*Comes down from the hill*)
Joshua! God told me that he will utterly put out the remembrance of
Amalek from under heaven.

JOSHUA
    (*Aggressively*)

That's what happens when you mess with the people of God! You get wiped out of existence!

MOSES
Uh … you okay, Joshua?

JOSHUA
(*Aggressively*)
Yeah, man, I'm good!
(*Exits stage*)

ISRAELITE 2
(*Exits stage*)

AARON
(*Comes down from the hill*)
I think he enjoyed fighting a little too much.

HUR
(*Comes down from the hill*)
Now what, Moses?

MOSES
Now I must build an altar, and call it Jehovah-nessi, because the LORD hath sworn that the LORD will have war with Amalek from generation to generation.

MOSES, AARON, and HUR
(*Exit stage*)

CREWMAN #6
(*Brings two chairs onstage; proceeds to exit stage*)

ACT 2, SCENE 6

The Twin Tablets

FRONT MAN

(*Continues reading*)

When Jethro, the priest of Midian, Moses's father in law, heard of all that God had done for Moses, and for Israel his people, and that the LORD had brought Israel out of Egypt; Then Jethro, Moses' father in law, took Zipporah, Moses' wife, after he had sent her back, And her two sons; of which the name of the one was Gershom; for he said, I have been an alien in a strange land: and the name of the other was Eliezer; for the God of my father, said he, was mine help, and delivered me from the sword of Pharaoh. Jethro had some advice for Moses.

JETHRO and MOSES

(*Enter stage*)

JETHRO

Moses? My favorite son-in-law. It's great to have you back here.

MOSES

Thanks for having me, Reuel.

JETHRO

For the last time, kid, it's Jethro now!

MOSES
Ha-ha … Hasn't it always been?

JETHRO
You better believe it. Anyway, after hearing everything about what happened with the Egyptians, I have a question for you.

MOSES
Ask away.

JETHRO
First take a seat.
(Sits down in chair)

MOSES
Don't mind if I do.
(Sits down in other chair)

JETHRO
What I wanted to ask was, what is this thing that thou doest to the people? Why sittest thou thyself alone, and all the people stand by thee from morning unto evening?

MOSES
Because the people come unto me to enquire of God: When they have a matter, they come unto me; and I judge between one and another, and I do make them know the statutes of God, and his laws.

JETHRO
The thing that thou doest is not good. Thou wilt surely wear away, both thou, and this people that is with thee: for this thing is too heavy for thee; thou art not able to perform it thyself alone.

MOSES
Are you suggesting I should write them down?

JETHRO
Well … yes. That would be a lot better. While you're at it, you should appoint able men to judge over the people as well. It'll make things easier on you. You know what—just make a whole pyramid of rulers. Rulers of thousands, rulers of hundreds, rulers of fifties, and rulers of tens: and let them judge the people at all seasons: and it shall be, that every great matter they shall bring unto thee, but every small matter they shall judge.

ZIPPORAH
(*Enters stage and pouts*)

MOSES
Good idea. I'll get right on it now.
(*Goes to exit stage but is blocked by Zipporah*)
Oh … hey!

ZIPPORAH
What? That's it? I don't see my husband for how many sunsets and that is all he can say to me?

MOSES
Hey … baby?

ZIPPORAH
I'll hey baby you!
(*Grabs Moses's ear and exits stage with him angrily*)

MOSES
Ow, ow. Look, I'm sorry. I was really busy …

(*Exits stage*)

JETHRO
(*Sniffles to audience*)
They grow up so fast.
(*Exits stage with both chairs in hand*)

FRONT MAN
(*Continues reading*)
Three months after the children of Israel left Egypt, they arrived in the wilderness of Sinai. When they camped by the mountain, Moses decided to go up into the mountain itself, in order to speak with God. There, God gave him a message for the people of Israel. He said that if they obey his voice and keep his words true to their heart, then he will make them a glorious treasure in his sight. Hence them being called God's people. Moses did exactly what God asked him to do, and the children of Israel said they would do exactly as Moses said God wanted them to. God told them to wash their cloths and prepare for the third day, because that was when he would come down from the mount and speak to them in a magnificent way. God also warned them not to touch any part of the mountain while waiting or they'd die … Ouch.

CREWMAN #7
(*Enters stage left holding up lightning bolts and cloud of light, has the tablets in pocket*)

MOSES
(*Enters stage right shaking*)
Everyone, out of your tent! The third day has arrived.

AARON
(*Enters stage right shaking*)

HUR, JOSHUA, and ISRAELITE 2
 (*Enters stage right shaking, gold in everyone's pocket*)

MOSES
Behold … the awesome power of God. The ground trembles, the skies
cry, the winds shatter, everything adheres to his voice.

THUNDERING VOICE
Come up.

MOSES, AARON, HUR, JOSHUA, and ISRAELITE 2
Okay.
 (*All start to walk stage left*)

THUNDERING VOICE
No!

MOSES, AARON, HUR, JOSHUA, and ISRAELITE 2
 (*Stop in their tracks*)

THUNDERING VOICE
Thou shalt come up, thou, and Aaron with thee: but let not the priests
and the people break through to come up unto the LORD, lest he
break forth upon them.

MOSES and AARON
 (*Walk stage left*)

CREWMAN #7
 (*Gives Moses the breakable tablets*)

MOSES and AARON
 (*Walk stage center and read it directly to the audience*)

MOSES
One: Thou shalt have no other gods before me.

AARON
Two: Thou shalt not make unto thee any graven image.

MOSES
Three: Thou shalt not bow down thyself to them, nor serve them.

AARON
Four: Thou shalt not take the name of the LORD thy God in vain; for the LORD will not hold him guiltless that taketh his name in vain.

MOSES
Five: Remember the Sabbath day, to keep it holy.

AARON
Six: Thou shalt not kill.

MOSES
Seven: Thou shalt not commit adultery.

AARON
Eight: Thou shalt not steal.

MOSES
Nine: Thou shalt not bear false witness against thy neighbour.

AARON
Ten: Thou shalt not covet thy neighbour's house, thou shalt not covet thy neighbour's wife, nor his manservant, nor his ox, nor his ...
    (*Looks at audience with a smile*)
Donkey, nor any thing that is thy neighbour's.

Moses and Aaron
(*Return stage left*)

Front man
(*Continues reading*)
God gave Moses that and more. He gave laws about murder, laws about animals, laws about personal belongings, laws about morality, laws about punishments, laws about feasts, and more. Moses was told to build a sanctuary of blue, purple, and scarlet and fine linen, and goats hair, and rams' skins dyed red, and badgers' skins, and shittim wood, including other materials.

Aaron
(*Walks stage right*)

Front man
(*Continues reading*)
He also spoke of a tabernacle, an alter, a courtyard by the tabernacle, offerings of oil, priest clothing, and consecrating Aaron and his sons.

Israelite 2
Aaron! What's taking Moses so long?

Aaron
He'll be just a minute.

Israelite 2
That's fifty-nine seconds too long! Here.
(*Takes out gold and takes gold from Hur and Joshua*)
Take our gold earrings, melt them, and mold them into a cow.

Aaron
Why?

ISRAELITE 2
Because we need a god to worship.

AARON
No, I mean, why do you guys have earrings?

HUR and JOSHUA
You got a problem with that?

AARON
Leviticus nineteen, verse twenty-eight, and Deuteronomy twenty, verse five.

ISRAELITE 2
Ha-ha. But we're still in Exodus.

AARON
Fair point.
    (*Takes gold and exits stage*)

ISRAELITE 2
What are you doing?

AARON
    (*Enters stage with small golden cow*)
I made the cow you asked for offstage.

ISRAELITE 2
Great! Now we can worship it.

THUNDERING VOICE
Go, get thee down; for thy people, which thou broughtest out of the land of Egypt, have corrupted themselves: They have turned aside quickly out of the way which I commanded them: they have made

them a molten calf, and have worshipped it, and have sacrificed thereunto, and said, These be thy gods, O Israel, which have brought thee up out of the land of Egypt.

MOSES
(*Walks stage right with breakable tablet*)
Aaron! What on earth is going on? I had to talk God out of destroying you all.
(*Sees cow*)
Is that a golden calf? Ah!
(*Breaks the tablet angrily, throws it to the ground, takes golden cow and throws it offstage*)

AARON, HUR, JOSHUA, and ISRAELITE 2
No!

AARON
What the heck, Moses? Those were the commandments.

MOSES
And you people are fickle, uncaring, and ignorant!
(*Grabs Aaron by the collar*)
What is the meaning of this, Aaron? You know this is against God's word!

AARON
They made me do it …

MOSES
(*Lets go of Aaron*)
Ye have sinned a great sin: and now I will go up unto the LORD; peradventure I shall make an atonement for your sin.
(*Walks stage left*)

Oh, this people have sinned a great sin, and have made them gods of gold. Yet not, if thou wilt forgive their sin—; and if not, blot me, I pray thee, out of thy book which thou hast written.

THUNDERING VOICE
Whosoever hath sinned against me, him will I blot out of my book.

MOSES
(*Walks center stage*)
The Lord wants us to continue our travel to the land flowing with milk and honey. He also said ye are a stiff-necked people.

AARON, HUR, JOSHUA, and ISRAELITE 2
(*Walk center stage*)
We're sorry.

MOSES
An apology implies that you carry a great deal of remorse and have no intentions of continuing these horrid acts. So I ask you, are you really sorry?

ISRAELITE 2
(*Exits stage*)

MOSES
(*Walks stage left*)

AARON, HUR, and JOSHUA
(*Walk stage right*)

ACT 2, SCENE 7

The Covenant

FRONT MAN
(*Continues reading*)
After the children of Levi came by Moses's side, they killed roughly three thousand men that worshipped the golden calf. Moses went away again for forty days. This time the Israelites that remained knew better than to disobey. God spoke directly to Moses while he was there. He told Moses to carve the commandments and laws again on a new set of tablets.

CREWMAN #7
(*Exits stage*)

MOSES
(*Exits stage*)

FRONT MAN
In his absence, Moses was shown God's back parts. Moses worshipped God and spoke with him there the whole time. After the forty days passed, Moses returned to the people of Israel.

MOSES
(*Enters stage with face light on, veil in pocket, and regular tablets in hand*)
Hello, everyone. How are you?

Aaron, Joshua, and Hur
(*Walk towards Moses and look directly at his face*)
Ah! So bright!

Moses
Huh? Oh sorry.
(*Covers face with veil*)
That should be better. All that time spent with God must have changed me a bit, huh?

Aaron
So what now, Moses?

Moses
We must build a tabernacle and pitch tents. We will worship God in here, and we must not drift away from his teachings. We must remember the Sabbath day, to keep it holy and never work on that day. Don't even light a fire. God is all the light we'll need. When in the tabernacle, Aaron and the other priests must wash their hands before entering to do their work. There will be many things inside the tabernacle, but be sure that no one, I repeat, no one touches the Ark of the Covenant.

Aaron
How will we do that, Moses?

Moses
I'm glad you asked!
(*Walks over to Front man and takes the big script he's reading from*)
Check this out.

EVERYONE
(*Enters stage, walks over to Moses holding the script, looks directly at script*)

MOSES
Let's go to work.
(*Begins to exit stage*)

CREWMAN #4
Wait, that's it?

MOSES
That's the end of Exodus at least.

CREWMAN #8
So what happens next?

FRONT MAN
The third book of the Bible.

ALL CREWMEN
(*Scratch their heads*)

FRONT MAN
Leviticus … it's not a trick question.

CREWMAN #1
Hey, boss.

FRONT MAN
What's up?

CREWMAN #1
(*Points at audience member*)

I think that guy was asleep through the whole thing.

CREWMAN #2
Great, now we have to do it all over again!

CREWMAN #3
Aw man! You gotta be kidding me.

CREWMAN #4
Did those death scenes mean nothing to you?

CREWMAN #5
I get paid by the hour so—

CREWMAN #6
You're getting paid for this?

CREWMAN #7
They'll all have to pay a second time if they want to see this again.

CREWMAN #8
I'll get the costumes ready …

FRONT MAN
No! No! *Noooo!* You want to know what happened? Here's what happened!

ACT 2, SCENE 8

Genesis and Exodus

FRONT MAN

In the beginning, God created the heaven and the earth, and then he created everything on earth, including man, whom he gave dominion over all things on earth. But man was lonely so God gave him woman. They both ate from the tree they were told not to eat from. They gained knowledge of good and evil and were kicked out, but God still loved them.

They have two sons, Cain and Abel. Cain kills Abel and runs away from God. The man and woman, Adam and Eve, in case you weren't catching on, then have a third son, Seth. Seth has children, Cain has children, and new nations are born because of their kin.

People being people refuse to accept God, so God tells a faithful man named Noah that he's going to flood the earth and start fresh with Noah. He tells Noah to build an ark that carries two of each animal, male and female. Noah and his family do so.

Years after the flood, the new nation of people start disobeying God again. Notice a trend here? They build a tower to see his face, so God gives them all different languages so they can't complete their blasphemous act.

Years after Noah dies, God appoints a man named Abram as the father of his covenant, but only after he changes his name to Abraham. Abraham has a son named Isaac. When God asks Abraham to sacrifice Isaac, without a question, Abraham obeys God and sends an angel down to stop Abraham. God rewards him for his obedience.

Isaac grows old and has twins named Esau and Jacob. Jacob betrays Esau, but God blesses Jacob as the better person. He promises to bless Jacob after he wrestles with an angel. Jacob has twelve sons and one daughter.

Joseph is his eleventh son and has dreams of being better than his brothers; his brothers get jealous and throw him in a well. Later they sell him off to Egyptians, but God still blessed Joseph and gave him favor in the sight of Pharaoh. After a bunch of tricks, his brothers realize it's him; he has two sons, Ephraim and Manasseh; and they are blessed with tribes.

Years later, a different Pharaoh wants all the newborn babies of the Hebrews killed. Thankfully God protects Moses as a baby and allows his mother to send him down a river. Pharaoh's daughter decides to keep Moses. He grows up and runs away from Egypt after killing an Egyptian. He meets his wife elsewhere but has to return to Egypt to free the people of God. After ten plagues fall on Egypt, Pharaoh lets the people of God go, but then he changes his mind once they've left. Pharaoh's men die on the way through the Red Sea. Moses travels with the people of Israel, who complain twenty-four seven even after Moses gives them what they ask for. Moses goes up Mount Sinai to be with God. God gives him the Ten Commandments. During one of his trips, he returns to see them worshipping a golden calf, or cow, as some might say. The calf worshippers are immediately killed. For obvious reasons, the ones that remain decide to stay devoted to God.

Moses is shown God's back parts and is told to continue his journey after building a tabernacle.

And the rest … is history!

EVERYONE

(*Takes a bow*)

Fin

About the Author

Ever since I was 8 years old, I enjoyed telling stories. I'd make funny stories, I'd make sad stories, but I was always told that I was an excellent story teller. Little did I know, this would hold true for the rest of my life. As an aspiring Pastor, I make it my mission to follow the will of God and not my own, showing my love by praying, fasting, reading his word regularly, and of course by honouring my father and my mother. They  were the first people to ever listen to my stories and would always give me an honest critique afterwards. For as long as I can remember, they always encouraged me to follow my dreams and aim to become what I wanted to be. The problem was, I didn't know exactly what I wanted to be in life. It was through high school, while taking drama classes that I realized what I really wanted to become. You see, I was writing scripts without abandon. The inspiration would hit me and I'd take off, and jot down the ideas. After school was over, I'd start to test some ideas for character interactions and settings. I just loved writing scripts. Some may have even said I was going crazy. To them I'd say "True love doesn't make you crazy, it keeps you sane." A lot of years and even more love was put into it, so I hope you love reading it, as much as I loved writing it.

Printed in the United States
By Bookmasters